STORIES IN STONE

PARK CITY, UTAH

MINERS AND MADAMS MERCHANTS AND MURDERERS

True stories of Park City's most colorful pioneers and maps to where they're buried

Author: Colleen Adair Fliedner
Photos: Kathie Kercher Horman

© *Flair Publishing, 1995*

Copyright 1995, Colleen Adair Fliedner. All Rights Reserved.

No portion of this book may be reproduced or used in any form, whether by print, magnetic media, electronic media, mechanical reproduction including photocopying, recording or any other information storage and retrieval system. Nor may it be used by any other means, without prior written permission from the author, except for the inclusion of brief quotations in a review.

First Printing: March, 1995

1 2 3 4 5 // 10 9 8 7 6 5 4 3 2 1

Manufactured entirely in the United States of America

Fliedner, Colleen Adair
STORIES IN STONE, Park City, Utah
Includes bibliographical references.
1. Rancho Los Amigos Medical Center Centennial
2. Stories In Stone, Park City, Utah

ISBN 0-9645742-0-9

Printed on post-consumer recycled papers.

The papers used in this book meet the requirements of the American National Standards for Information Services - Permanence of Paper for Printed Library Materials, ANSI Z39.48 - 1984

Flair Publishing
4141 Ball Road, # 446
Cypress, CA   90630

CONTENTS

NAME	PAGE #	MAP #
PREFACE	v	
ACKNOWLEDGEMENTS	vi	
INTRODUCTION	vii	
1902 MINE DISASTER VICTIMS	28	PC 30
BENNETT, FRED & CLARISSA	36	GW 16
BERRY, MARTHA & EDWARD	37	GW 38
BERTZ, PETER	38	GW 37
BETTINGER, DAISY	38	GW 45
BLOMGREN, NELS	39	GW 6
BRANNAN, MATHEW	2	PC 7
CHRISTENSEN, JENS	39	GW 23
CLARK, JOHN FELIX	39	GW 2
COLLINS, MARTHA	2	PC 9
COONEY, JOHN	3	PC 12
COONEY, MARTIN & PETER	3	PC 11
COUGHLIN, PATRICK	40	GW 40
CRIB, (BABY)	4	PC 14
CROWLEY, MICHAEL	41	GW 52
CUNNINGHAM, MARY	41	GW 27
DALEY, BABY	4	PC 19
DALTON, ANDREW	42	GW 41
DeGROVER, D. L. H.	5	PC 31
DIEM, BABY	42	GW 29
DON, WILLIAM	43	GW 54
DUNBAR, WILLIAM BRUCE	43	GW 34
DUNSMORE	44	GW 5
EVANS, E. P.	6	PC 23
FARISH, JOHN H.	44	GW 26
FLETCHER, BLANCHE	45	GW 1
FOX, ANN E.	46	GW 18
FUELLING, HOPE	7	PC 4
GASPARAC, JOSEPH	8	PC 32
GIBSON, ANNIE & THOMAS	9	PC 37
GIBSON, JOHN	46	GW 39
GIBSON, MYRA WYCOFF	10	PC 24
GIDLEY, ANNIE & WILLIAM	48	GW 32
GITTINS, ALVIN	10	PC 41
GLENWOOD CEMETERY	35	GW
GLENWOOD CEMETERY MAP	35A, 35B	GW
HARRISON, HARRY	48	GW 8
HAYS, CHARLES	11	PC 6
HOAR, BABY	12	PC 18
HOAR, WILLIAM	12	PC 33
HOVER, ANNIE	49	GW 14
HUGHES, JOHN	50	GW 28
JONES, WILLIAM "BLINKO"	50	GW 25
JUDGE, JAMES	13	PC 26
KEARNS, MARY ELLEN	14	PC 5
KENNEDY, JIMMIE	51	GW 7
KESCEL, EMMA LOUISA	14	PC 20
KILFOYLE, SARAH & ANDREW	15	PC 22
KIMBALL, GILBERT	17	PC 35
KIMBALL, ROBERT	16	PC 35
LANGTON, ALEX	51	GW 48

iii

CONTENTS

NAME	PAGE #	MAP #
LOCKHART	52	GW 36
MACDONALD	52	GW 31
MAWHINNEY	53	GW 19
McBRIDE, HENRY	18	PC 29
McCORMICK, WILLIAM	53	GW 24
McDONOUGH, BARTLY & MINNIE	54	GW 4
McFALL	18	PC 8
McFARLANE, JOHN	57	GW 8
McLAUGHLIN, WILLIAM & JOHNNIE	55	GW 44
MILLER, WILLIAM & HANNAH	56	GW 46
MITCHELL, ROBERT	57	GW 12
MOTT, CLYDE	58	GW 35
MOYN, ELLA	58	GW 42
NELSON	19	PC 10
NELSON, WILLIAM "JENKS"	20	PC 10
NIMMO, JOHN	58	GW 30
NORMAN, FREDERICK	59	GW 13
NORTHEY, DAVID & JOSEPH	60	GW 50
O'KEEFE, JOHN	61	GW 51
O'KEEFE, MARIE	21	PC 40
PAPE	61	GW 10
PARADISE, LEWIS	62	GW 47
PARK CITY CEMETERY	1	PC
PARK CITY CEMETERY MAP	1A, 1B	PC
PETERSEN, RAY & EVA	63	GW 9
QUICK, JAMES	63	GW 3
QUINN, JAMES	22	PC 28
RICHARDSON, GEORGE	22	PC 25
ROARK, MARION	23	PC 13
ROSEVEAR	64	GW 21
RYAN, MICHAEL & JOHN	23	PC 39
SHIELDS	64	GW 20
SIMMONS, SAMUEL	65	GW 33
SMITH, A. M. B.	66	GW 49
SMITH, GEORGE	24	PC 21
SNYDER, GEORGE	24	PC 1
SYNDER, PEARLE	26	PC 15
SYNDER, RHODA	25	PC 16
STREET, HOWARD	67	GW 17
STRINGER, MATILDA	27	PC 34
STRINGER, THOMAS	67	GW 22
TOWEY, JAMES	68	GW 43
TROTMAN	29	PC 36
TROTMAN, PATRICK MILTON	31	PC 2
TRUSCOTT, HARRIET	68	GW 53
URBAN, RACHAEL	31	PC 27
WALKER, WILLIAM	32	PC 17
WARD, MOLLIE ALLEN	33	PC 3
WATSON, P. B.	69	GW 55
WILLIAMSON, EDWIN	69	GW 15
YATES, CLAUDE	34	PC 38
ZUCCA, JOSEPH	70	GW 11
CHRONOLOGY	71	
SOURCES	74	

PREFACE

Park City, Utah, sits like a jewel in the Wasatch Mountains; a world-famous ski resort located a convenient 33 miles from downtown Salt Lake City. Charming and serene, Park City is an enchanting 19th century mining town where expensive homes dot nearby aspen and pine covered hillsides.

Like the thousands of other people who visit Park City each year, I was intrigued, captivated by the old town's charm. Year after year I returned, drawn back to a place where the present meets the past in a most delightful way. And each time I came, I found myself strolling through the two cemeteries...the places where the people who actually lived the history lie at rest.

Curiosity about who these people were, and how they lived and died finally got the better of me. I began researching their stories--first in Park City, and finally moving into the archives in Salt Lake City. Information was scarce, a little like finding the proverbial needle in a haystack. But I was able to piece together the lives of some very fascinating people.

STORIES IN STONE will give you a glimpse into the lives of some of Park City's most controversial and interesting residents. Because space constraints prevented me from using all of the stories and photographs, I begrudgingly selected only those people whose accomplishments, both good and bad, provided the most historical data.

Even though this book centers on the more "sensational" stories, most of the residents of Park City were ordinary people who lived everyday lives. They loved and laughed; they cried and mourned. They went to Saturday night dances or to the theater, had dinner with friends in local restaurants, and attended church on Sundays. They looked forward to the annual Fourth of July parade, the big sale at the local clothing store, and the day the new toys arrived at the mercantile for Christmas. They fell in love and were married, had children and all too often buried them. They felt joy and pain just like we do today.

As a historian, I've come to realize that people are people--the dates and fashions may change, but the people certainly do not. It is to these men, women, and children, who lived and died in Park City, that I dedicate this book. Tread lightly as you walk through the two cemeteries...for here sleep the people who built this lovely little town in the mountains.

(Author's Note: While the maps are your guide to their grave sites, there are a few instances where I've included a story about someone whose grave we weren't able to locate. But because I felt the person was so fascinating and/or important to the city's history, I couldn't bear to leave the story out. Please feel free to write me if you locate one of these lost grave sites so that I can add it to the records.)

ACKNOWLEDGEMENTS

The amount of material providing details about the individuals in Park City and Glenwood Cemeteries is sparse at best. Without the diligent efforts of the Park City Historical Society and the residents of Park City, it is doubtful enough data would have been available for research historians to study. Thus, I wish to thank Hal Compton, Mary Anne Cone and the rest of the staff at the Park City Historical Society for their assistance and advice, as well as their unrelenting work to keep Park City's past from being forgotten.

I would also like to thank the following: Bea Kummer for her years of valuable record keeping which provided great insight into Park City's fascinating history; and most especially Valeska Spears, Park City Parks and Recreation Department, for providing valuable maps and cemetery records; the staffs of the Family History Library in Salt Lake City and Park City's Public Library for their assistance and beneficial resources; and Dr. David Chan and Dr. Kathleen Whitaker for their expertise and input.

Above all, a heartfelt thank you to my right arm and research assistant, Vicki Treu of Salt Lake City, who spent countless hours tromping through the two cemeteries, combing through the microfilmed newspapers and historical data, and doing research in the genealogical records. And, finally, thank you to the photographer and assistant extraordinare, Kathie Kercher Horman of Sandy, Utah, for her wonderful photographs and her many trips to Park City's cemeteries to search for missing headstones. Without Vicki and Kathie's assistance, it would have been impossible to complete this book.

INTRODUCTION

Park City's story begins with the discovery of the first mine in the late 1860s. Word of the silver strike quickly spread through the United States, crossing the oceans to Great Britain and Europe. Prospectors and miners began streaming into the Wasatch almost immediately--slowly at first, but as other ore outcroppings were discovered, the slow trickle became a torrent of human beings immigrating to Park City from all over the world. Each man came with dreams of instant wealth and a better way of life. Although Park City's mines produced a handful of millionaires, most of the dreamers ended up working for someone else, chipping away at rock hundreds of feet below the surface of the earth.

One of the earliest encampments sprang up around Lake Flat (now known as Silver Lake). Another settlement grew along a fork of Silver Creek in Deer Valley. The miners lived in tents or brush shanties which had been haphazardly thrown together as shelter from the bitter cold. While these camps were convenient for working in the mines, accessibility to the outside world was difficult at best, and in the heavy winter snows, it was impossible. Miners found themselves snowbound for weeks, even months at a time.

In 1872 several families established a settlement in the lower hills, in an area which received less snowfall and was easier to reach from other settlements and towns. The camp soon evolved into a small town, and they gave it the name "Park City." As the years passed, most of the people living in the higher elevation camps moved into the thriving new town. Names like Snyder, Street, Evans, Nelson, and Kimball became Park City's first families, building stables, boarding houses, and mercantile stores. Virtually every type of business imaginable came to Park City: Bakeries and confectionery stores, a butcher shop, restaurants, theaters, dance halls, and clothing stores. Unfortunately, with the trappings of a mining town came the saloons (at one time there were 27), along with gambling, prostitutes, murders, shootings and lynch mobs. With goods and services readily available, and jobs in the mines abundant, the population burgeoned to over 3,500 by 1880 and to about 7,000 by the mid-1890s.

While the mines were the backbone of the economy, they were a double-edged sword. Providing jobs for thousands of men, and more than 450 million dollars in silver to the nation, they also spilled poisonous run-off into local streams. Smoke spewing from the smelters and mills frequently blanketed the town. Stamp mills, like the one located on the east side of town behind Main Street, crushed rock from the mines at a deafening ninety-four times a minute. The heavily forested mountains were soon stripped of timber to be used in the mines, leaving behind barren hillsides.

Indeed, Park City was far from the picturesque resort town that it is today. In 1894, the *Park Record* newspaper reported that the streets were continually torn up for repairs, and that the town was constantly without water "...to say nothing of water being furnished that would poison a hog." It goes on to say that many lives had been lost because of the bad water. "The evil from which this camp has suffered since its foundation must be remedied." Cemetery records list many people who died of all sorts of cancers, and the local pollutants might have been the cause.

Life in the old mining town was difficult. Naturally, the main occupation was hardrock mining. Accidents were frequent...and deadly. Miners rarely saw the light of day, breathing dust and quartz particles that lodged in their lungs. Silicosis, or miner's consumption, killed many of Park City's miners, including the famous John Judge, a real rags-to-riches millionaire who started out as a miner and wound up owning large interests in Park City's mines.

Epidemics of diphtheria, typhoid fever, smallpox, and influenza were common. City officials attempted to stop the spread of these diseases with quarantines, but with only marginal success. For instance, in the world-wide Spanish flu epidemic of 1918, all public places were closed and people were advised to stay indoors as much as possible to avoid the sickness. While the number of deaths in Park City wasn't as high as in some other cities, many people still died from this flu.

Another attempt at stopping the spread of an epidemic was in 1888 when smallpox broke out in town. This was terribly contagious, so a "pesthouse" was built in Empire Canyon to confine those people who were infected with the disease. Many died in spite of the quarantine, although the newspaper reported there were actually more fatal cases of diphtheria during the smallpox epidemic.

There were several newspaper articles reporting that there were shortages of medicine in Park City. Epidemics were at their worst during the winter months, and this was when heavy snowstorms made the roads impassable. Replenishing local medical supplies or getting the sick or injured patients into a well-equipped hospital in Salt Lake City was nearly impossible.

Between the pollution, rampant disease, freezing winters, avalanches, frequent cases of pneumonia, and mining accidents, was it any wonder there were so many deaths in old Park City?

In the very earliest years of pioneers and prospectors, makeshift graves were dug in the hillsides without much regard to placing the deceased in an established cemetery. For those who were too poor to be taken to Salt Lake City or over to a cemetery in one of the other valleys, anywhere would have to do. This is easily understood when one considers the distance a body would have had to been transported to get to the nearest cemetery.

During the 1860s, a small cemetery was laid out in Snyderville, and another was started at the Mormon meeting house near Kimball Junction. But these cemeteries were still miles from the mountain camps, so the miners finally established their own cemetery on a sage-covered hillside in what is now Deer Valley. Some 19 of the town's first pioneers were laid to rest there.

But as the majority of the population shifted down to Park City, it became clear that the new town needed its own cemetery. This happened quite by accident when Pearle Snyder, the infant daughter of one of the town's most prominent families, died in the winter of 1879. George and Rhoda Snyder had attempted to take the child's body to a cemetery out of town. But a winter storm made their trip impossible, so they buried Pearle on a hillside in their pasture. Ironically, this tragedy was the beginning of the town's first graveyard, Park City Cemetery. A second cemetery, Glenwood, was opened in 1885 as a burial place for members of Park City's ten or more fraternal organizations.

PARK CITY AND GLENWOOD CEMETERIES

One of the first things you'll notice when walking through either cemetery is the large number of children's graves. Park City's child mortality rate was exceptionally high. It was common for a mother to give birth to eight or ten children, and then lose all but two or three, as in the case of the Hales children buried in Glenwood Cemetery. Nonetheless, it was still a hellish nightmare for the parents of yesterday to have one of their children die. Inscriptions, like "Darling Pet," "Budded on Earth to Bloom in Heaven," "Our Darling Babes," and "One Sweet Flower has Drooped and Faded," serve as reminders of the human emotion, the grief these people experienced when losing a child.

You'll also observe that there are many large family plots that contain one or two children's graves, and you will no doubt wonder why the parents aren't there. Park City has never been a ghost town, but its population has fluctuated dramatically with the price of precious metals. Families who had lived here for decades were forced to leave when the mines closed down, moving elsewhere in search of work. It must have been difficult for these people to leave their loved ones behind.

While the rows of monuments in the two cemeteries stand as silent reminders of Park City's harsh past, some are quite unique and actually beautiful. Many are very ornate, with delicate ferns, birds, draped tapestries, and even logs carved into the limestone or granite. Much of the stone for these monuments came from the quarries in the east and were ordered from Summit Monumental Works, which distributed a free catalogue. Still others are simple headstones, etched with names and dates, and may have been obtained in Salt Lake City.

Researching these two cemeteries posed a special set of problems, as there were countless inaccuracies made by the early record keepers. The most prevalent error was the omission of names from the official cemetery records. Dozens of burials weren't recorded in both cemeteries. Names were often misspelled. Other names were listed, but no plot number was recorded. Many times only one or two names are listed when entire families are buried in that location.

The records kept by the city-appointed sexton (now housed in the Family History Library in Salt Lake City) don't match the burial records turned over to the Park City Parks and Recreation Department. Glenwood's only existing records are also incomplete. But with the help of my hardworking assistants, **Kathie Horman** and **Vicki Treu,** we were able to locate many of the unrecorded graves by walking through the cemeteries countless times. Occasionally, we couldn't find a headstone, even when the sexton's or other records showed its location. I have concluded that they had wooden markers which must have disintegrated over the years, or that the person was buried without any grave marker as a cost-cutting measure.

While it appears there has been a great deal of vandalism in Glenwood, many people believe that the damage may have occurred during the construction of local condominiums. The headstones were covered by a deep layer of snow when heavy equipment drove through the cemetery, knocking over and crushing some of the concealed tombstones. However, because so many markers have vanished, it's likely that some vandalism has occurred in past years. The one exception would be the children's headstones topped with a small lamb, which can be seen in both cemeteries. These lambs were so delicate, so fragile, that pieces have simply broken off during the passage of time. Decades ago a woman complained to the *Park Record* that she had merely touched a lamb's head, when its ear crumbled like salt in her hand.

STORIES IN STONE focuses on the most prominent or controversial men and women in Park City's history, as well as those who died tragic deaths. Sensational stories, such as the mine explosions, have always received more attention by the press. And rich, prominent men were written about with greater frequency than their wives. Thus, I was able to gather more information about these people than the everyday people who lived normal lives and died of "old age."

Rich and poor, immigrant and native-born American, Protestants and Catholics--they were all buried in Park City's cemeteries. Through the decades, memories of these people have faded, and their stories have been forgotten. As you walk through the cemeteries and read about their lives, it is hoped that some of their stories will reach into the hearts and imaginations of the future generations who will visit Park City.

PARK CITY CEMETERY

Park City Cemetery is situated on a wind-swept hillside just below town. Its beginnings date back to 1879, when George and Rhoda Snyder buried their daughter, Pearle, on a south-facing slope of their pasture. Later, the Snyders reportedly deeded the land over to the city. In November of 1891, a new ordinance called for city officials to purchase land adjoining the "old cemetery," and to have it plotted, numbered, and fenced. The new area was to be called the "City Cemetery." A sexton was appointed to dig graves and keep the records.

The west end, the oldest section of the cemetery, was originally named "Mountain View," and includes the graves of some of the town's most beloved and famous citizens. The name was later changed to the "Park City Private" Cemetery, which likely occurred in 1891 when the connecting public City Cemetery was opened. On the other hand, the miners jokingly called City Cemetery "Gidley's Pasture!," a name which undoubtedly made Sexton William Gidley cringe.

No one knows how many unmarked graves are still in the lower portion of the west end where many people buried at county expense were believed to have been interred. There are still a few decaying wooden planks visible...but wood decays quickly in the extremes of weather experienced in Park City.

Maintenance and record-keeping of the 40-acre cemetery are under the jurisdiction of the Park City Parks and Recreation Department. Although it's a historic site, the cemetery is still in use. Please use caution when walking up the hills, and, as a visitor to this peaceful place, please respect those who rest here.

Take Park Avenue (Hwy. 224) to Kearns Blvd. (Hwy. 248). Turn east away from the ski lifts. The cemetery is on your left.

PARK CITY CEMETERY

1 - GEORGE SNYDER
2 - PATRICK MILTON TROTMAN
2 - MANY UNMARKED GRAVES
3 - MOLLIE ALLEN WARD
4 - HOPE FUELLING
5 - MARY ELLEN KEARNS
6 - CHARLES HAYS
7 - MATHEW BRANNAN
8 - McFALL
9 - COLLINS
10 - NELSON
11 - MARTIN & PETER COONEY
12 - JOHN COONEY
13 - MARION ROARK
14 - CRIB (BABY)
15 - PEARLE SNYDER
16 - RHODA SNYDER
17 - WILLIAM WALKER
18 - BABY HOAR
19 - BABY DALEY
20 - KESCEL
21 - GEORGE SMITH
22 - KILFOYLE
23 - EVANS
24 - WYCOFF - GIBSON
25 - GEORGE RICHARDSON
26 - JAMES JUDGE
27 - RACHAEL URBAN
28 - QUINN
29 - HENRY McBRIDE

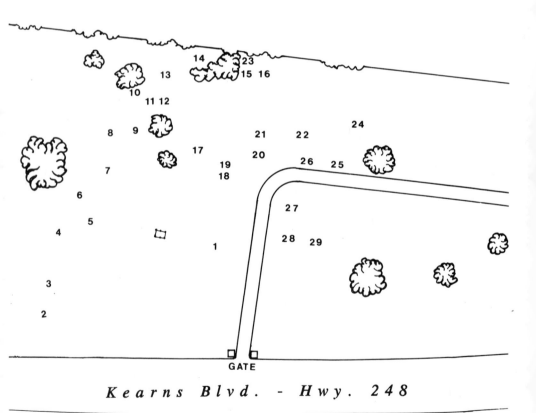

Kearns Blvd. - Hwy. 248

PARK CITY CEMETERY

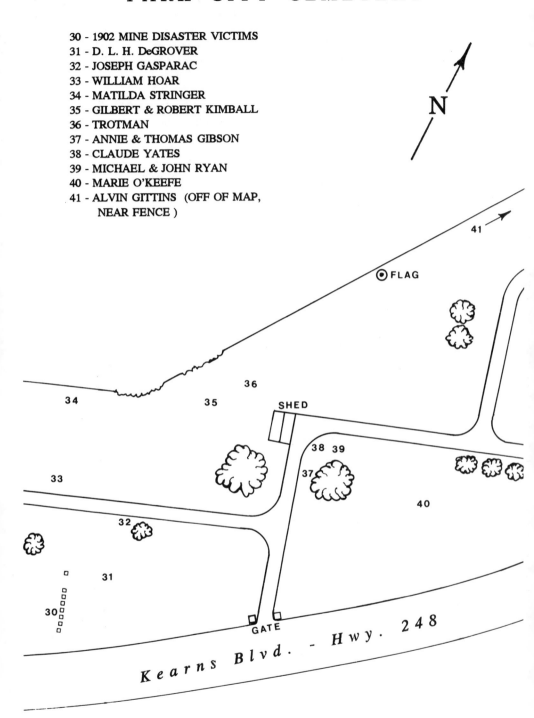

- 30 - 1902 MINE DISASTER VICTIMS
- 31 - D. L. H. DeGROVER
- 32 - JOSEPH GASPARAC
- 33 - WILLIAM HOAR
- 34 - MATILDA STRINGER
- 35 - GILBERT & ROBERT KIMBALL
- 36 - TROTMAN
- 37 - ANNIE & THOMAS GIBSON
- 38 - CLAUDE YATES
- 39 - MICHAEL & JOHN RYAN
- 40 - MARIE O'KEEFE
- 41 - ALVIN GITTINS (OFF OF MAP, NEAR FENCE)

STORIES IN STONE

MATHEW BRANNAN   Map: PC 7

The story of Mathew Brannan's murder is one of the best known stories of a rough and tumble time in Park City. It was August 22, 1883, when Matt was shot from his horse while riding to check on his claim in Iron Canyon. He lived long enough to relay that it was the infamous Black Jack Murphy who'd pulled the trigger. Murphy surrendered to the sheriff, but hostile Parkites prompted authorities to move Black Jack out of town. They thought he'd be safe in Coalville, but they were wrong. A lynch mob from Park City hijacked the Utah Eastern train and headed for Coalville. They demanded Black Jack Murphy, and were accommodated without a fight! The vigilantes took him back to Park City for hanging. When dawn broke the next day, Black Jack's body was swinging from a pole alongside the railroad tracks. It's most likely that Black Jack was laid to rest in the city cemetery--but you won't find his marker anywhere. Either his grave was marked with a wooden plank--the cheapest kind of marker--or it wasn't marked at all. After all, Murphy was buried at county expense, and like so many other criminals, he received the quickest and cheapest burial.

Brannan's funeral procession was accompanied by a cornet band, and the grave-side services were performed by the local Odd Fellows chapter. Mathew Brannan's monument is broken, and half of it lies on the ground.

MARTHA COLLINS   Map: PC 9

Martha Washington Collins was one of the many Parkites who died of the Spanish Influenza pandemic that claimed millions of lives in 1918. Martha was born in Park City in 1893, graduating from the local high school in

1914. She had dreamed of being a nurse, of helping people. At the time of her death in 1918, she was studying nursing in Ogden while working at Dee Hospital. Her body was taken to the City Cemetery for burial, but because of the quarantine regulations, no public gatherings were allowed. Thus, Martha's parents weren't permitted to have a funeral service.

She rests in the private section of the cemetery with her parents, Daniel and Ellen, as well as several siblings.

MARTIN & PETER COONEY   Map: PC 11

The Cooney Brothers, Martin and Peter, were six years apart in age. Martin died in 1895 at the age of 59, and Peter lived until 1898. The cement-like logs symbolize their profession and their affiliation with the Woodmen of the World organization. Both monuments are very unusual and, although it's possible they were cast in cement, they've both held up to the weathering process nicely.

The only historical records that mention the name Cooney list a Mrs. Catherine Cooney as the proprietor of a candy store in Park City. Most likely, she was the wife of one of the Cooney brothers.

JOHN COONEY   Map: PC 12

Not far from the Cooney brothers lies another Cooney named John, who may have been Martin and Peter's cousin. John, fondly known throughout town as Jack, died in 1905 when he was only 34. The doctor suspected typhoid fever, but after he was hospitalized, rheumatism developed, settling in his heart. Although Jack had lived in Park City for ten years, he wasn't a member of any of the secret societies or fraternal organizations. He had worked as a blacksmith for the American Flag mine and was also the business manager of the Banjo Club which was organized in December of 1896. The newspaper reported he left a substantial insurance policy ($500) to his wife, Lena Stoll Cooney, a local Park City girl whom he married on September 23, 1899.

BABY CRIB   Map: PC 14

At the top of the hill not far from Marion Roark's bench-like marker, where the groomed, grassy area ends and the brush begins, you can find one of the most unique monuments in Park City's cemeteries. Rusting, twisted wire forms a shape that resembles a baby's bassinet. When it was new, it was most likely painted white and was a beautiful grave marker for its tiny occupant. However, as the years have passed and nature has taken its toll, all that remains is a sad, nameless gravesite, a touching tribute of the love felt for the infant by the heartbroken parents.

BABY DALEY   Map: PC 19

"Baby" Daley's headstone is situated in an area of the City Cemetery in which many babies were buried. The fact that the child wasn't named would indicate it died during birth.

Baby Daley was the child of well-known Parkite Frank Daley, superintendent of Park City and Midnight Sun Mining Company. In 1902 Frank began working for the mining company, replacing Foreman Duncan Gills, who was killed when he fell down a mine shaft. Frank Daley continued working in this position for more than 20 years. Unfortunately, nothing could be located about the baby's mother.

Park City Cemetery

D. L. H. DeGROVER   Map: PC 31

One of the last of the Chinese immigrants in Park City was D. L. H. DeGrover. No one really knows how many Chinese resided in Park City in the early days, but it's estimated that at one point there were around 300 living in the gully east of Main Street. Early accounts of the arrival of the first Chinese in Park City are foggy at best, but the old timers used to say that the "Celestials" (an old slang term for Asians) had been there almost from Park City's very beginning. They had worked in the mines of California and Nevada, and had built the west's railroads. Many came to Utah for jobs in the gold diggings at Brighton and Alta. But when word of the silver strikes swept around the world like a wild fire, they streamed into Park City hoping to find new opportunities.

The Chinese weren't welcomed in Park City's mines any more than they had been welcomed anywhere else. This was a time of great anti-Chinese sentiment, and violence towards them was all too frequent. This was because the Chinese worked for lower wages and were often used as strike breakers. Park City's entrepreneurs knew that if they employed Chinese to work in the mines, there would be trouble. So, they hired them as laundrymen, cooks, and domestic servants to work in the mine-owned boarding houses.

As you wander through the cemetery, you may notice the conspicuous absence of Chinese headstones. The grave of D. L. H. DeGrover is the only Chinese burial left in Park City, in spite of the fact that there were once scores of Chinese grave sites. While there were no records kept of these burials, the newspaper is filled with descriptions of festive Chinese funerals complete with firecrackers, music, feasting and a noisy entourage waving colored strips of paper while enroute to the cemetery. According to Chinese custom, however, the bodies were eventually disinterred and returned to China for burial in Chinese soil...with one notable exception: D. L. H. DeGrover.

Dong Ling Hing DeGrover (or Quom Nom Low, depending on which story you read) called himself, "Mr. Grover," a name the Anglo-Parkites could pronounce more easily. Reportedly, this was the name of a man DeGrover admired greatly, Grover Cleveland, president of the United States. Born in San Francisco in 1857, D. L. H. DeGrover was one of the last Chinese businessmen remaining in the city after the turn of the century. He apparently decided to stay in Park City because he owned a great deal of real estate all over town.

DeGrover had a wife and son whom he supported back in China, returning to his native country frequently to visit them. But after his wife's death, he brought his son, Joe, back to Park City. D. L. H. DeGrover died of pneumonia in 1926. Ironically, his funeral was held at the Community Church, which was filled to capacity with his friends. There was none of the customary Chinese celebration; instead, a solemn Christian church service was held for "Old Grover," a man who was admired and highly respected by the people of Park City. He was 69 at the time of his death. D. L. H. DeGrover must have loved his adopted town in the Wasatch Mountains, as he never wanted his remains to be returned to China.

Joe DeGrover, who inherited his father's fortune, continued to live in Park City for another 30 years.

E. P. EVANS   Map: PC 23

The son of Parley P. Evans, one of Utah's early Mormon pioneers, Edward Evans was born in Centerville, Utah, on September 5, 1862. In spite of the Mormon church's request that none of its members participate in the practice of mining, Edward went to California to search for gold. But like most prospectors, he was unsuccessful; so Evans returned to his home in Utah.

However, in 1880, when stories of Park City's silver strikes filled the newspapers, Evans moved to the mining camp, working for the Ontario

Park City Cemetery

Company. Evans eventually left the mines to pursue a business career, opening a local livery stable. He also managed the Hopkins Coal Company from 1895 until well after the turn of the century. Evans became one of the town's most prominent citizens, and by 1902, he had been elected to serve as Park City's mayor. E. P. Evans died on January 1, 1933.

Edward met a local girl, Lillian Snyder (the daughter of George and Rhoda Snyder), and the couple was married in 1885. Lillie bore nine children; however, only three survived. Lillie, who was born in 1866, died in 1938, outliving Edward by only five years.

The Evans family rests on the hillside of the Park City private section.

HOPE FUELLING   Map: PC 4

It was a pleasant Sunday afternoon that fateful day in April of 1892. Seventeen-year-old Hope Daisy Fuelling was walking alongside the Utah Central Railroad track about a mile from the station. She was on her way to the Trotman ranch to join her mother when she ran into Lewis Paradise. Was it an accidental meeting or a tryst the pair had pre-arranged? Apparently, Hope's parents had warned her about seeing Lewis Paradise and felt that he was a bad influence on their daughter. Besides, Hope was engaged to another man, Fred Witten, who was in Germany on business.

Patrick (nicknamed Patsy) Milton Trotman, age 27, was Hope's uncle (her mother's brother-in-law). Trotman and Paradise had heated words at the Dexter Livery Stable (operated by the Kimball Brothers) a short time prior to Paradise's scheduled rendezvous with Hope. When Lewis left, Trotman followed him. As the couple strolled together, Lewis'

7

arm around Hope's shoulder, Trotman watched from behind a bush, becoming more and more enraged. Leaping out of the shrubbery, he began firing his pistol. The first bullet, intended for Paradise, whizzed between the pair. Lewis ran for town, while Trotman pursued the girl, firing two more shots. When the authorities arrived, they found that Trotman had laid down next to the mortally wounded Hope and turned the gun on himself. He was still alive...just barely. But Hope was dead.

The Fuelling family, who had settled in Park City in 1881, owned the City Bakery and Candy Kitchen on Main Street and lived in the rear of the building. Hope's body was brought home in a wagon and laid out on the family table, while a friend went to get her mother, who was still at the Trotman's ranch.

Patrick Milton Trotman lingered for a number of days before dying. Ironically, he, too, was buried in the Park City Cemetery. However, either his grave wasn't marked because of the town's outrage, or his wooden grave marker has rotted into obscurity.

Was this a crime of passion? Hope's father expressed his shock that Trotman was romantically interested in his daughter. Or was it merely that Trotman was an over-protective uncle? We'll never know the truth.

Hope was born on September 28, 1874, in Wathena, Kansas. She lies in the private section of Park City Cemetery. Many other Fuelling family members are buried nearby.

JOSEPH GASPARAC   Map: PC 32

In March of 1913 there was an accident at the Silver King Coalition mine. But this time, it wasn't an explosion or a cave-in, the two most common disasters experienced in Park City's mines. Joseph Gasparac and another miner, L. W. Lasser, were asphyxiated when they ran into deadly poisonous gases, which the miners called the "white damp," at the 1300-foot level of the Silver King. Rescuers, wearing gas masks to protect themselves from the fumes, arrived too late. Gasparac was found slumped over some equipment, while his assistant, Lasser, was lying on the ground.

Joe Gasparac was born in Croatia in October of 1890, coming to America in 1909. He moved to Park City in 1912 to work in the mines, and married a local girl, Jennie Lake, four years later. The couple had lost a baby, Rachael, in January of 1923, just a few short months before Joe's death. He left behind four other young children.

There was a large group of Croatian immigrants in Park City. Gasparac was a member of the local lodge of Croatians, as well as a member of the Maccabees.

ANNIE M. & THOMAS N. GIBSON   Map: PC 37

Born in 1871, Annie Gibson grew up in Park City. As an old woman, she often shared her memories of Park City's early mining days. Annie spoke of the pollution caused by the mining operations that caused a dense smoke to hang over the valley. The chemicals in the fumes were so caustic, they ate holes in the laundry the women hung out to dry and etched the glass windows in their homes. She also remembered the little stream running through Main Street named Silver Creek. It was crystal clear and filled with trout back when Annie first came to Park City as a child. But as the years passed and the mine shafts honeycombed through the mountains, run-off from the mine companies found its way into Silver Creek. The water became so polluted that the Parkites called it "Poison Creek."

She married Thomas Gibson, a miner, and the couple moved to Ontario Canyon to raise their family. A witness to decades of history, Annie lived a long, interesting life. She died in 1960 at the age of 89. Annie lies buried beside Thomas, who died three years later.

Annie and Thomas Gibson's flat headstone is etched to resemble an open book, an appropriate symbol for a woman who left so many memories behind for others to share.

February, 1913: There was an outbreak of contagious diseases. Many people believed it was because the water was not allowed to settle and clarify before it went into the city mains. A committee was formed to look into the matter. More rigid quarantine regulations were recommended.

STORIES IN STONE

MYRA T. WYCOFF GIBSON   Map: PC 24

The 24-year-old wife of Alex Gibson, Myra Wycoff Gibson was expecting a child. But it was a difficult pregnancy complicated by a liver ailment. She began convulsing, and the infant was born dead at 4:30 a.m. on April 10, 1909. Myra hung on for another half hour, and then slipped away.

When walking through the myriads of headstones in the old cemeteries, it's easy to believe that death was such a frequent visitor to Park City in those days, people would have become accustomed to losing loved ones. No where is this misconception more evident than in the story of Myra's death.

Her father, Jacob, had been sick. Upon hearing about the death of his beloved daughter and her baby, he became so despondent, his friends said the poor man simply gave up on life. He, too, was dead within 48 hours...dying of a broken heart.

It was a triple funeral. Myra, her baby buried in her arms, lies in Park City Cemetery next to her father, Jacob, and her mother, May. The fact that Myra was a member of Women of Woodcraft would indicate her husband was a member of the Woodman of the World, and that he was employed by one of the local mines. Myra was born in Gold Hill, Nevada, and came to Park City in 1896 with her parents. She married Alex Gibson in 1906 at the age of 21. Alex isn't buried with Myra and the baby, and it's unknown what happened to him.

ALVIN GITTINS   Map: PC 41

On March 7, 1981, Park City mourned the passing of Alvin Gittins, a well-known artist who was born in Park City in 1922. Gittins was especially renowned for his self-portraits and realism. Gittins, who began painting at the age of 18, taught at the University of Utah until his untimely death.

In 1981 an art show was scheduled at Kimball Art Center featuring the work of Alvin Gittins. Sadly, the internationally-renowned artist died just days before its opening.

Park City Cemetery

(Due to space limitations, this grave is off the map--almost against the fence, past the flagpole.)

Gittins said: "I am fascinated by man and woman and living things...their flesh and bone, their folly, their beauty, their variety. If I could reflect these things strongly, and down to the last significant gesture or wrinkle, perhaps I could also reveal a meaning veiled, yet expressed by the surfaces of life; then I would be content."

(From *The Newspaper*, March 5, 1981)

CHARLES HAYS

Map: PC 6

Charlie Hays and his wife, Maggie, had a new-born baby. The young couple had lived in Salt Lake City, where Charlie worked for Germania Lead Works, until he got a better paying job up in Park City in the Daly Mine. Charlie moved into the mine's boarding house, while Maggie stayed in Salt Lake until the spring thaw. Finally, it was May 25--moving day for Maggie and the baby. Ironically, it was the same day 23-year-old Charlie died.

Charlie went to work that morning, carrying his candle and a sack of gunpowder. When he reached the

STORIES IN STONE

700-foot level of the Daly Mine, something went wrong. An explosion rocked through the mine. John Judge found what remained of poor Charlie, who had literally been blown to pieces.

Speculation was that somehow Charlie's candle ignited the powder, though no one knew for sure. The mine company paid for his grave and headstone. Maggie and the baby stayed in Salt Lake City.

BABY HOAR   Map: PC 18

In what used to be the private section of Park City's cemetery lies "Baby" Hoar. The tiny grave is enclosed by a wooden frame which someone has filled with plastic flowers. No dates were given on the simple white plank, and cemetery records didn't even record the child's burial. The fact that the infant didn't have a first name would indicate that it died at birth.

Baby Hoar was one of the children of William and Eliza Hoar, who were married in Park City in 1895. The Hoars had six children, but two had died by 1910. William, who was born in 1868, died in 1914 and is buried in another section of the cemetery. (See Map # PC 33)

What's interesting is that both William and Baby Hoar's wooden grave markers are of the same shape and style. Both are painted white with black letters. Because William died in 1914, a wooden marker would have decayed decades ago. Thus, a surviving descendant must have had new, matching markers made for father and child sometime more recently. Baby Hoar's grave is on a hillside dotted with the graves of children and infants, a sad epitaph to Park City's high child mortality rate.

Park City Cemetery

Another William G. Hoar is several rows east of William Hoar. This was the son of William and Eliza, and the brother of Baby Hoar. One of Park City's many World War I veterans, William G. Hoar died in 1920.

JAMES JUDGE   Map: PC 26

Born in County Sligo, Ireland, in 1833, James Judge was the brother of millionaire John Judge, one of the owners of the Silver King Mine. Unlike his brother, James Judge was never rich or famous, but worked as a foreman at the Daly Mine. When John Judge became wealthy from his mining interests, he moved with his family to the Salt Lake Valley and built a palatial mansion; however, brother James remained in Park City, raising his five children and participating in the city's government.

At the age of 61, James Judge died of pneumonia, a common ailment with a high fatality rate. James and his wife lost a 20-year-old daughter named Norah, who is buried beside her father. However, James' wife isn't buried there, either remarrying or leaving Park City.

Around 40% of all cases of pneumonia ended fatally. It was considered a "bad air" disease which occurred mainly in the winter when people got little fresh air. Getting fresh air day and night, even if quite cold, was very important in treating the disease. Patients with pneumonia were advised to avoid overeating and to sit in a very hot bath. Lung congestion could be relieved by swallowing large doses of salt mixed in a little water. If the patient was thin and anaemic, heat should be kept on the chest. But if he was "full-blooded," an ice bag was applied to the chest as soon as he'd cooled down from the bath. Then the entire chest, front and back, was wrapped with a "pneumonia jacket," consisting of a thick layer of absorbent cotton saturated with olive oil and covered with oiled skin or muslin.

STORIES IN STONE

MARY ELLEN KEARNS   Map: PC 5

Born in Ireland in 1893, Mary Ellen was the three-year-old daughter of William and Catherine Kearns. The child's body was discovered 300 yards down river from her family home in Empire Canyon. It was believed she slipped and fell in Silver Creek, which ran across the Kearns' property.

This may have been one of the many relatives of Thomas Kearns, one of Park City's millionaire miners.

EMMA LOUISA KESCEL   Map: PC 20

Certainly one of the most beautiful monuments in either of Park City's cemeteries is the tiny replica of a Roman Temple which was erected for Emma Louisa Kescel, wife of James T. Kescel. The Kescels were from England and were residing in Park City by 1880. It's believed that James was Park City's first marshal and was also a street commissioner in 1880. Earning $125 per month, James' salary was quite good for that era.

Emma was born in 1855 and died in 1899. A large Episcopal service, complete with a choir and a eulogy read by the Dean of St. Mark's Cathedral in Salt Lake, was held at the graveside. It was an Eastern Star funeral service, an organization in which Mrs. Kescel was quite active.

Two Kescel children, Louisa and William, lie nearby. Louisa died in 1881 at the age of five months, and William died in 1884 at two years of age. James is not buried in the family plot. Many years later, two of the Kescels' surviving children, Minnie and Joe, became involved in Park City's fledgling ski industry.

SARAH E. & ANDREW KILFOYLE   Map: PC 22

Born in Nova Scotia on June 24, 1838, Sarah arrived in Utah in 1855 with one of the first waves of Mormon pioneers. It was in the burgeoning Salt Lake Valley that she met and married Andrew L. Kilfoyle, also from one of the original Mormon families. Andrew L. Kilfoyle was born on November 23, 1831 in Warwick, Canada. The couple was married in 1857.

Like many other Mormons, the Kilfoyles moved into the high mountain meadows east of Salt Lake to raise livestock for the church, building a large ranch about a mile below Park City. Records show that prior to 1897, before the Mormons had built a chapel in Park City, baptisms were conducted at the Kilfoyle Ranch.

One of Sarah and Andrew L. Kilfoyle's daughters, Laura, married William Trotman, a union which would bring terrible grief to the Kilfoyle family. Laura's niece, Hope Fuelling, (see the Fuelling & Trotman stories) was murdered by her maternal uncle, Milton Trotman (Laura's brother-in-law). Three weeks later, Andrew L. Kilfoyle, Sarah's husband, died.

The Kilfoyle monument is a gabled obelisk near the fence. Note that the name Andrew W. also appears on the back of this headstone. This was the son of Andrew L. and Sarah, who died on November 21, 1893, a little more than a year after Andrew L.'s death. He was only 25. So, within a two-year period, poor Sarah lost her husband and a son.

Tragedy struck again in 1902 when William Trotman, Laura's husband, tried to kill his entire family (see the Trotman story). Most likely, Sarah helped Laura raise her children after their father fatally shot himself.

According to both her obituary and cemetery records, Sarah Kilfoyle died on July 18, 1914, at the age of 76 and was buried with her husband and son in the City Cemetery. However, her headstone is missing, although it's obvious there is an unmarked grave next to the Kilfoyle monument.

Besides being active in the L. D. S. church in Park City, Sarah Kilfoyle was known for "lending a helping hand" to anyone in the community who needed assistance.

STORIES IN STONE

The Kilfoyle name is also important in the George Snyder story, as two of Snyder's wives were Kilfoyles. Caroline and Martha Kilfoyle Snyder were the sisters of Andrew L. Kilfoyle.

ROBERT TAYLOR KIMBALL   Map: PC 35

Born in 1857, Robert Kimball was the son of William Henry Kimball, eldest son of Heber C. Kimball, one of the early leaders of the Mormon Church.

Robert's father, William, had been in the business of owning and running stagecoach lines most of his life. Robert grew up at the Kimball family's way-station, an eleven-room structure built by his father along the Overland Stage route. The large stone building was constructed at the stage stop located about a mile east of Kimball Junction, and was touted as one of the finest way-stations along the Overland Trail. All of the Kimball children helped run the way-station--taking care of the horses, catching fresh trout for the guests' dinner, and attending to the myraid of chores that came with running a way-station of this size. For decades, the Kimball Hotel served as an Overland Stage and Wells Fargo Station, and was reputedly a stopping place for government dignitaries.

Robert left home when he was thirteen and began his first venture into the world of business when he was hired by the Wells Fargo Company to bring a large herd of cattle to Parley's Park from Evanston, Wyoming. This was a most amazing feat for the young man, particularly when you consider that Robert did it single-handedly. But Robert was tenancious, seemingly following in his father's determined and ambitious footsteps.

Robert Kimball's adventures included a trip to Arizona with his father, where they helped set up another stage line. While there, Robert was part of a group of investors who set up the township of Mesa, Arizona. Later, he traded his Arizona interests for full ownership of the Kimball Brothers Saloon, located in the Kimball Hotel in Parley's Park.

In June of 1883, William Kimball's stagecoach business had grown immensely, and he finally turned the Park City to Salt Lake Line over to his sons, Robert and Burton. The boys changed the name from the Park

City & Salt Lake Stage Line to the Kimball Brothers' Pioneer Stage Line, dropping the word Pioneer many years later.

The Kimball Brothers' stagecoaches ran on the road between Salt Lake City and Park City until the railroad made them obsolete. The stage line closed in 1890, ending a chapter in Park City's history. Then in 1900 Robert and another brother, Lawrence, bought the Dexter Livery and Feed Stable on the edge of town, selling wagons and horses, as well as boarding horses for the day. By 1903, Robert even managed the Park City Ice company.

Not only was Robert Kimball one of Park City's entrepreneurs, he was active in many civic affairs. For instance, the old records list him as one of the first trustees of the town's schools.

Robert died in 1934 at the age of 77. His wife, Amanda Evans Kimball (one of the Park City Evans family), lies by his side, while many other Kimball children are buried in various areas of the Park City Cemetery.

GILBERT KIMBALL   Map: PC 35

Gilbert John Kimball was the son of Robert and Amanda Evans Kimball (see above). Gilbert was born on July 17, 1899, about the time the railroad came to Park City, when the Kimballs closed the stage line and got into the livery stable business. Gilbert lived in Park City most of his life, dying in 1983. His flat grave marker shows that he had been a Private in the U. S. Army.

Gilbert Kimball lived through more than 80 years of world history. A child at the turn of the century, he witnessed both world wars, the popularization of the automobile, the birth of aviation, and the first man in space. He lies beside his mother and father in Park City Cemetery.

FROM AN 1890 NEWSPAPER AD:

LAXATIVE BROMO QUININE TABLETS CURE A COLD IN ONE DAY. NO CURE, NO PAY. PRICE 25 CENTS.

STORIES IN STONE

HENRY McBRIDE   Map: PC 29

Working in the mines was a strenuous, hazardous, and difficult job. Henry R. McBride took a few days off of work to vacation in Salt Lake City. In spite of the fact that it was late February, he went to the indoor Municipal "bath pool" for a swim. No one was sure exactly what had happened, but witnesses said that Henry was acting strange and that he had struggled in the water for a few moments. Then he began to float lifelessly. When he was pulled out of the pool, Henry was already dead. Officially, it was ruled failure of the heart. This was strange, indeed, when you consider that Henry was only 24 years old. The year was 1923.

Born on August 1, 1899, Henry was a native Parkite. He was a member of the L. D. S. Church, where funeral services were held as soon as his body could be shipped back to Park City. He lies buried in the City Cemetery next to his mother, Emma, and his father, Cyrus R. McBride.

McFALL   Map: PC 8

Another prominent family in Park City's early history were the McFalls. Charlie McFall came to Park City in 1881 with his wife, Mary Stout, whom he'd married in 1876. Charlie, who was an active member of several lodges, had been employed by the city for four years in various capacities. He died on Christmas Day, 1890, of kidney problems. The McFalls lost infant twin sons, Allan and Avis, in 1888. Another son, Ralph, died in 1891.

Note that the monument is made of cast bronze, as were all of the footstones for each family member.

Park City Cemetery

NELSON

Map: PC 10

On the side of the hill, resting beneath the shade of a towering pine tree, the Nelson family slumbers in a large plot. A memorial plaque lists the names of each family member. The patriarch of this family, Colonel John A. Nelson, provides us with an especially interesting story.

John Nelson had served as a cavalry colonel in the Indian Wars, and when he first came to Park City in the early 1870s, he served as a U. S. Marshal. Like the Snyders, one of the other pioneering families, the Nelsons operated a boarding house catering to the miners. Mrs. Nelson (Eliza Cunningham Nelson) ran the boarding house while John roamed the hills to prospect. He eventually discovered several ore deposits, including what later became the Park Nelson, Nelson Queen, and the Woodside and Tenderfoot mines.

Sometime before 1880, he sold at least part of the lucrative Woodside and Tenderfoot claims to a man named E. P. Ferry. The Woodside became part of the famous Silver King mine, one of the world's largest silver producers. Apparently, the sale didn't make Nelson as wealthy as some of his prospecting peers, but he did manage to live off of his investments. John, who died at the age of 45 in 1880, was one of the first people buried in the City Cemetery.

One of Col. Nelson's claims to fame involved the darkest incident in Utah's history, known as the Mountain Meadows Massacre. As the U. S. Marshal, Nelson oversaw the execution of John D. Lee, who was one of the leaders of this massacre. Nelson wound up with Lee's personal possessions, including several journals. These fascinating materials were later donated to the renowned Huntington Library in Southern California.

STORIES IN STONE

The Nelson's family home was in an area once known as Nelson Hill. After the turn of the century, Mrs. Eliza Nelson donated a portion of the family's land on which the Miner's Hospital was built in 1904. The hospital was later moved to its present location (near Park Ave. and 13th Street). The Silver King Hotel is now situated on the spot originally occupied by the Miner's Hospital, and the Nelsons' property has been incorporated into Park City's ski resort.

The Nelson marker shows the names of all but one of the family members. Colonel Nelson's son, William, later known as "Jenks Nelson," became one of Park City's most colorful characters. (see below) Jenks, who died in 1954, was the youngest of the Nelson children. (Note that Eliza bore a daughter, Nancy, the same year that she lost her husband and was left to raise the children alone.)

WILLIAM H. "JENKS" NELSON   Map: PC 10

On May 5, 1954, one of Park City's most interesting, cantankerous, and delightful citizens died. William Nelson, better known as "Jenks," was certainly a colorful character in Park City's history. (Jenks Nelson was no relation to another local character named "Pop Jenks.") Nelson had been a military man, a captain in the Spanish-American War of 1898. This was how he earned his nickname--it had come from a song, "Captain Jenks of the Horse Marines." Nelson was pleased that he was identified with the lyrics and readily adopted the name Jenks. He wore his uniform proudly for the rest of his life, riding his horse through Park City's streets long after the other residents had taken to the automobile...and long after he was no longer in the military. Jenks Nelson was a commanding, albeit frightening figure to the local children, who, as adults, still recall his spirited cursing and rough-and-tumble manners.

William Jenks Nelson was the only surviving child of Colonel John Nelson. Most peculiar are the contradictions between the information contained in the census materials and Nelson's obituary. According to the newspaper, William Nelson was born in Salt Lake City in 1876. However, the 1880 census shows that William was six years of age that year, which means he was born in 1874. Also, the obituary states that Jenks Nelson came to Park City in 1882, but other documents say that his family moved to Park City in the early 1870s. In fact, Col. John Nelson, his father, made one of the earliest mineral discoveries, so it's very unlikely that the Nelsons came to Park City as late as 1882.

At the time of his death, William Jenks Nelson was still active in both civic and mining affairs. In fact, even at his advanced age, he was the president of the Park Nelson Mining Company, which was located in the Blue Ledge Mining District. One of his father's discoveries, this was one of the mining claims left to him.

Jenks Nelson never married and out-lived virtually every other member of his large family by many years. He spent most of his life living alone on the family ranch, reputedly a beautiful chunk of land filled with groves of aspens and natural springs. His ranch has since been cleared and incorporated into the ski runs of Treasure Mountain.

Jenks Nelson died of "old age" at Miners Hospital--a fitting place for him to die, as the hospital was built on land donated by his family in 1904. Jenks' obituary says that he was buried in the Park City Cemetery. Oddly, Jenks doesn't have a headstone in the family plot, in spite of the fact there was plenty of room for him next to his sister, Lila. Either he was too obstinate to buy his own headstone, or he was laid to rest in another section of the cemetery. There is no record showing the actual location of his grave. Since Jenks never married, he left no children behind to tell us where he lies at rest. But, it's highly likely he's there with the rest of the Nelsons under the big tree on the hill.

MARIE O'KEEFE   Map: PC 40

Mrs. Marie Hethke O'Keefe lived in Park City for around 60 years, during which time she was the manager of several local hotels. Her first position was in the hotel located in the old Maple Hall which burned in the Great Fire of 1898. After that she went to work as the manager of Mr. Miller's Park City Hotel (see William Miller's story). But as luck would have it, that hotel also burned down in 1912. So, Marie became the proprietor of the New Park Hotel until her retirement in 1952...at the age of 78.

(Incidentally, the New Park Hotel is now "The Claimjumper.")

Many of Park City's old-timers still fondly remember Mrs. O'Keefe hustling around the New Park Hotel, directing the cook in the back kitchen, stirring a pot on the big gas stove, or making sure the hotel guests were comfortable. Marie, who died at the age of 84, lies beneath a simple headstone in the Park City Cemetery. It's unknown whether Marie O'Keefe had any children, as she's not buried with any family members.

JAMES QUINN   Map: PC 28

One very sad tale to tell is the story of James Quinn, a successful businessman in town. Quinn was a partner in the Quinn & Hyde Livery, besides owning a great deal of mining stock. On September 9, 1897, something went wrong in James' otherwise happy life. He was married and had several small children, but business was bad; so bad, apparently, James planned his suicide and the murder of his wife.

James was so calloused and calculating about his heinous plan that he actually stopped by the barber shop for a trim and a shave on his way home. Naturally, no one suspected what he was about to do. When he finally arrived home, he asked his wife, Ellen, if she had any last remarks to her children. Ellen was confused, answering that she didn't know what he meant. A moment later, in front of their children, James pulled a pistol from his coat pocket and shot her point-blank in the head. Then he turned the gun on himself.

Most remarkable is the fact that they buried James next to his victim. Poor Ellen must remain by James' side...with him for all eternity, just as he wanted.

GEORGE RICHARDSON   Map: PC 25

George Richardson was one of the volunteers who entered the mines to rescue victims of the explosion at the Daly-West which claimed 34 lives on

Park City Cemetery

July 15, 1902. Like many of the other town "heroes," George didn't even work in the mines.

In spite of the dangerous fumes that filled the Daly-West and Ontario tunnels, seventeen-year-old George rode the rescue cage to the bottom and brought bodies to the surface. Unfortunately for George, he made one too many trips down the shaft. His body was later found about 70 feet down an incline of the mine shaft. Though he was dead, George was standing erect, his arm still suspended around an air pipe. He, too, became a victim of the mines.

MARION F. ROARK   Map: PC 13

Three-year-old Marion F. Roark died on July 19, 1879. It's believed this is the second oldest grave in the cemetery. Little Marion Roark was the son of Lawrence Roark, an Irish miner who came to Park City in the first wave of prospectors in the 1870s.

The cemetery records don't go back this far, so we don't know how the child died. Because the camp was constantly ravaged by typhoid fever and diphtheria epidemics in the late 1870s, it's likely the child died of one of these diseases.

The bench-like sandstone monument is reminiscent of the type found in many cemeteries in Britain. However, it's the only one of its kind in either of Park City's cemeteries.

MICHAEL A. & JOHN J. RYAN   Map: PC 39

Michael "Mike" Ryan was born in Perty, Kansas on February 24, 1884. Michael and his brother, John J. "Jack," came to Park City in 1918. They eventually opened a cobbler's shop, the "Park City Shoe Hospital," which was located in the old Grand Hotel building. This was no ordinary shoe shop--it was a place where the townsfolk often gathered socially, dropping by to catch up on the latest news of the day.

Another brother, Pat Ryan, served as Park City's sheriff for a number of years. Later, around 1930 Pat was working as the custodian of Jefferson school.

Michael died in 1930 of an illness complicated by a cold when he was only 46, while John lived to the advanced age of 81, dying in 1953. The brothers' parents, John and Bridget Ryan, are also interred in the City Cemetery.

GEORGE W. SMITH   Map: PC 21

Well-known Parkite and member of the law firm of Smith and Brim of Park City, George W. Smith was killed in an auto accident in May of 1918. The Smith family, accompanied by several friends, were on their way to Heber to visit other Smith family members living there. About 1-1/2 miles from town (near Begg's Mill), George made a sudden turn which sent the car out of control. It flipped over, pinning George under the steering wheel. Several passengers were thrown clear, while two others, including an infant, were also under the car. However, they all survived. George wasn't as lucky.

George Smith, former mayor of Park City, was born in Charleston, Utah and came to Park City when he was a boy. For more than 14 years he had been a volunteer fireman, and had served as city treasurer for a number of years. George and his family were Mormons, living at 909 Park Avenue. Other Smiths buried in the plot in the City Cemetery are his son, George A. (1908-1919) and a daughter, Georgia, who died in 1917 when she was only three months old.

GEORGE GIDEON SNYDER   Map: PC 1

The son of Lovisa Comstock and Isaac Snyder, George Gideon Snyder was born on June 11, 1819, in Palmyra, New York. The Snyders were early converts to the Mormon Church, and they eventually moved to Nauvoo, Illinois, when George was 19 years old. Two years later, the family relocated to St. Joseph, Missouri, where George met and married Sarah W. Hatch.

Park City Cemetery

In 1849 George and Sarah brought their two children to the Salt Lake Valley, but it was only a temporary move. When word of the gold strikes in California spread to Salt Lake City, George took his family to the west and mined for gold. Four years later, they returned to Utah. Just how much gold George pulled from the rivers and mines of California is unknown. However, shortly after his return to Salt Lake City, he took a second wife, Elsie Jacobs. A year later, he married Caroline Kilfoyle in 1856. (Caroline Kilfoyle's name can be seen on George Snyder's monument and lies by his side in death. Caroline died in 1889, two years after George.)

Sarah died that same year, so George married wife number four, Martha Kilfoyle, in 1857. He served a two-year mission for the Mormon Church in England between 1858 and 1860. One cannot help but wonder what happened to his wives while he was gone.

By far, the wife that is most remembered in Park City's history is Rhoda Shadwell Orchard Snyder, who became George's fifth wife in 1865. (Rhoda was 23 years younger than George and lived to the ripe old age of 84. She's buried up the hill from George and Caroline. See Map # PC 16.) In 1868 the Snyders moved once again...this time to Silver Creek in Summit County, but that was only until George heard the news that there had been a rich strike at the Emma Mine in Alta. George bought wagons to haul ore, while Rhoda ran a boarding house which the couple opened not far from the mine. When news reached George Snyder about the big silver deposit in Parley's Park, however, he packed up the family and moved once again to the mining camp that would later be called Park City. That was in 1872.

Being a man of foresight and substantial wealth, George bought up large parcels of land in Park City, including the area on which the Park City Cemetery was later built. He owned and operated the first livery stable in town, as well as barns which housed the ore and freight wagons for the mines.

Some people say it was Rhoda who named the town, "Park City," while others credit George with this honor. For the most part, before the Snyders arrived, the town had been inhabited by men. Most were miners--single men who lived in the boarding houses provided by the mines.

"Aunt Rhoda," as she was called until the day she died, opened a boarding house of her own, feeding her guests with her delicious home-cooked meals. The site for this boarding house was at the corner of Park and Heber Avenue where Kimball's Art Center is now located.

Since there wasn't a doctor in the camp, Rhoda nursed the sick. It's believed that George's other living wives were each given a ranch outside of town, as Rhoda was supposedly the only woman in town during the early years. She was highly respected and well-liked by the miners.

Rhoda Snyder gave birth to the first baby born in Park City, Sherman M. Snyder, in 1874. Sherman, who died at the age of 28, is one of the many Snyder family members buried in the City Cemetery. (This conflicts with other accounts which state that their daughter, Pearle, was the first baby born in Park City. However, Pearle wasn't born until 1877, about three years after Sherman's birth.)

George Snyder is credited with building the first grist mill in Summit County, Utah, and was active in political, church and business affairs. He was a rancher, raising some of Utah's finest horses. In 1865 Utah's Governor Doty appointed Snyder as a probate judge, an office which he filled for three terms. George lived an interesting life, a life filled with adventure and success. He died after a six-week-long illness at the age of 67, leaving behind 34 children and scores of grandchildren, many of whom are also buried in Park City Cemetery.

PEARLE SNYDER   Map: PC 15

Baby Pearle Snyder became ill just before the Christmas of 1878. With no doctors in the area at that time, there was little that Rhoda, the infant's mother, could do to nurse Pearle back to health. Sadly, the one-year-old girl died on February 22, 1879.

George Snyder made a tiny casket for the baby's body, and he and Rhoda headed for Salt Lake City to bury her. It was a particularly heavy winter that year, and the roads were impassable. When they couldn't get to Salt Lake, George and Rhoda tried for Heber City. By now, snow was falling in blinding drifts. Just about the time they were ready to give up and return home, Rhoda saw a patch of dry earth where the afternoon sun beat down on the hillside. Digging a hole, George and Rhoda laid their tiny daughter to rest in the desolate plot of land they used for grazing cattle in the warmer months.

They had intended to dig up Pearle's coffin after the spring thaw and transport her down to the cemetery in the Salt Lake Valley. But Rhoda just couldn't do it. She and George deeded the property over to the city for a local cemetery, and other burials soon followed. Many of the city's most prominent citizens were buried in Park City Cemetery.

Pearle Snyder was 19 months old at the time of her death. Though her pink sandstone monument is worn, the letters are still legible. It reads: "IN MEMORY OF PEARLE. DAUGHTER OF GEO G & RHODA SNYDER. DIED FEB. 22, 1879, AGED 1 YEAR, 7 MOS. 8 DAYS." Note Pearle's footstone--it has a little star on it, with her initials "P.S." and the date 1879.

Most likely, Pearle died of diphtheria, as there were diphtheria epidemics during the winters of both 1879 and 1880.

MATILDA STRINGER   Map: PC 34

Matilda Stringer survived her husband, Thomas Stringer, by around 18 years. Thomas Stringer, who was one of the local assayers, is buried in Glenwood Cemetery with numerous Stringer children. Matilda had lived in Park City for nearly 40 years. But after her husband's death in 1911, she moved to San Francisco, California to live with her daughter, Lillie Cochran.

Matilda died at Lillie's home after a six-week-long illness on August 7, 1929. She was 64 years old.

Matilda was born in Sweden in 1865 and came to Park City with her family when she was a child. It was here that she met Thomas, fell in love, and was married. Matilda was an active member of the Order of Rebecca's, the women's organization which was the counterpart of the Oddfellows.

Lillie had accompanied her mother's body back to Park City for burial. Tragically, Lillie, died in Park City shortly after Matilda's funeral. The newspaper reported that Lillie had been weak and distressed over the loss of her mother and suddenly keeled over while at the home of a friend. Her body was returned to her husband in San Francisco.

The mystery is why Matilda isn't buried in Glenwood with her husband and children. The newspaper obituary states that she was indeed buried in Glenwood; however, she was buried in the Park City Cemetery...up the hillside from William Hoar towards the fence.

THE DAY THE TOWN MOURNED.   Map: PC 30

Everyone in Park City lived in fear of an explosion in the mines. It had happened many times. But by far, the worst mine disaster in Park City's history occurred on July 15, 1902.

The explosion was believed to have occurred when the powder magazine at the 1200-foot level of the Daly-West was accidentally ignited. Not only were many men burned by the heat of the blast, but scores more were killed by the deadly poisonous fumes that began to spread through the labyrinth of tunnels that honeycombed through the mountains. By the time the final count was made, 34 men had died, many of whom were volunteers trying to rescue their fellow Parkites.

This neatly aligned row of headstones represents eight of the 34 men lost that day. The Daly-West and Ontario Mines buried all of the men at company expense as a gesture of good will. These eight men were buried together in a massive funeral unlike any other in the town's history. They were all Catholics from Ireland.

Park City Cemetery

One of the men, twenty-two-year-old Richard Dillon, was a volunteer who died after bringing the bodies of numerous victims to the surface. On a return trip into the mine shaft, he began to feel dizzy and became unconscious. Unfortunately, his companions tried to carry him out, but they, too, had become faint and were forced to leave him behind. Richard had just arrived in Park City from Ireland. Ironically, he had rescued his father, who worked in the mines, from a cave-in only two weeks earlier.

Brothers Harry and John Devlin had come to America together, and they died together while working at the 1400-foot level of the Daly-West Mine. Harry was 25 and John was only 23.

Most of the 34 victims were buried in Park City or Glenwood Cemeteries. Whenever you see July 15, 1902 as the date of death, it was most likely one of the men who died on that terrible day.

TROTMAN   Map: PC 36

According to both the sexton's and Park City Cemetery records, this is where William "Roy" and Laura V. Kilfoyle Trotman were buried. In spite of the fact that their headstones are gone, I wanted to include the Trotmans' stories. I'm sure you'll agree they were a fascinating family.

The Trotmans had more than their share of troubles. Two of the Trotman brothers, Patrick and William, had tragic deaths. In 1902 William Trotman and his wife, Laura, lived just outside of town. William had been unstable for some time and was finally institutionalized in a mental hospital in Provo. When he was sent home, however, he was far from well. Still in a deep depression, William sneaked out to the tool shed and got a large wrench. He crept into the bedroom where two of his daughters, Pearl and Emiline, were sleeping, and tried to kill them, hitting them on their heads with the wrench. When Laura heard their screams, she ran into the room to stop William, while the couple's 10-year-old daughter ran to a neighbor's house for help. But Laura couldn't stop him, and he began to beat her, too.

Suddenly realizing he had failed in his heinous mission, William dropped the wrench, grabbed his rifle, and ran out into the yard. A moment later he put the barrel to his heart and pulled the trigger. By the time the authorities arrived, 47-year-old William was dead. The newspaper reported that William Trotman had told a friend he was worried that insanity ran in his family, and that he would rather see his daughters dead than risk having them wind up in an aslyum one day. Thus, the despondent father had decided to take their lives. The date was September 6, 1902.

It must have been difficult for Laura to cope, but she and the children continued to live in Park City. Perhaps she returned to live with her aging mother, Sarah Kilfoyle, at the family's ranch. (She's shown in the census as a farmer, so it's likely she moved from her small home to a large piece of property.)

Cemetery records list "Roy" Trotman as Laura's husband and the three girls' father. However, the newspaper called him "William." So, one might conclude that William used the nickname Roy. On the other hand, there is a Roy Trotman listed in the 1910 census as the seven-year-old son of the widow Laura Trotman. This would mean that 36-year-old Laura was pregnant with the boy when her husband died, and that she named her son Roy. Could the Roy Trotman buried here be Laura's son?

As for the girls, Emilie (or Emiline), who was born in 1882 and was 16 at the time of this terrible tragedy, later went to work in a local bakery as a clerk. She also worked as a servant for one of the more well-to-do families in town. Pearl recovered from her severe head injuries. She eventually married William Green, dying of influenza in 1922 at the age of 44. Pearl's marker is a pretty flat stone painted with two red roses. (See Map # PC 22, near Kilfoyle's monument.) Emilie Trotman, who married John Quintana, is buried next to Pearl.

Another sad tale was the story of William's brother, Patrick. Patrick Milton Trotman murdered his niece, Hope Fuelling, before turning the gun on himself (see the Hope Fuelling story). Patrick, known as Patsy, was born in Doniphan County, Kansas in 1865, and died on May 11, 1892 of a self-inflicted gunshot to his forehead. According to the Sexton's Cemetery Records in Salt Lake City, Patrick Trotman was buried in the Park City Cemetery; however, his grave number was not recorded, nor is there a headstone marking the site. Most likely, he was buried in an unmarked grave at county expense in the section reserved for paupers, thieves, and other "undesirables" (probably, the lower west portion of the cemetery near Kearns Blvd., Map # PC 2).

The Trotmans were one of the numerous Mormon families that came into the area during the 1860s to raise cattle. Many of the Trotman men also held jobs in the sawmills of Snyderville. There are several Trotmans buried in the small cemetery in Snyderville, including another William Trotman. This couldn't be the same William Trotman married to Laura, as L.D.S. Church records show that this man moved into the area before 1860 as an adult. Laura's husband, William, wasn't even born until 1855. So, this must have been an ancestor of the Park City William Trotman.

RACHAEL URBAN   Map: PC 27

Perhaps one of the most colorful people buried in Park City Cemetery is Rachael Urban, one of the town's madams. Rachael was married to George Urban, a carpenter from Denmark. The couple was married in 1898 when Rachael was 35 years old.

Rachael and George came to Park City from Ohio just after the turn of the century. It's unknown when the Urbans decided to open their brothel, but by 1910 Rachael and George were operating a bordello on Heber Avenue using 8 to 10 girls. (Originally the brothels were on Main Street, but in 1907 an ordinance was passed to keep the "soiled doves" a more respectable distance from town.)

Mother Urban, as the miner's often called her, was a generous woman who often gave money to local people in times of need. According to some people, "Mother Urban" had a wooden leg and walked with a cane. Rachael, who weighed well over 200 pounds, often sat on her front porch near her large parrot, which sat on his perch and swore at passers-by. And when she came into town, she was driven by a uniformed driver in a limousine!

Rachael was born in Ohio and bore a total of six children. Five of the six had died before 1910, and the last child, Richard Urban, lies buried in the plot with George and Rachael. So, it would appear Rachael left no heirs. Another man, Peter Howarth, who died in 1915 at the age of 59, was also buried with Rachael and George. Was this a family friend or a relative that the good-hearted madam buried at her own expense?

Although she died in 1933 at the age of 70, Rachael Urban is still remembered by Parkites as the city's most famous madam.

WILLIAM "PLUM-BOB" WALKER   Map: PC 17

William Walker was murdered on January 22, 1883, while he was working in the yard of his home near the bottom of Main Street.

It seems that someone shot him from a barn across the street. The *Park Record* article added that Walker was survived by two wives and 31 children and that "murder is definitely suspected!"

Walker received the name "Plum-bob," because he searched for ore with a Spanish dip-needle--a device resembling a plumb bob. The old prospector was 68 at the time of his death.

Park City Cemetery

MOLLIE ALLEN WARD   Map: PC 3

On the morning of March 15, 1923, the body of 35-year-old June St. Clair was found. She had been brutally murdered by Pedro Canno, a local miner. Canno had stabbed her through the heart, and by the time the police arrived, she was already dead. The poor woman had pulled the knife from her breast and was still clutching it even in death. The motive for the murder was believed to have been robbery.

June St. Clair, whose real name was Mollie Allen Ward, was a prostitute who lived in the "crib"--or red light district--on Heber Avenue (now Deer Valley Road). Mollie called herself Pearl Ward, and later when she was a "lady of the night", she chose the name June St. Clair, a glamorous pseudonym she no doubt used to protect her real identity.

Mollie Ward came to Park City from Oregon around 1920. It was here that she met and married Charles Ward...a union which ultimately ruined her life. Mollie worked in town as a fashion designer and seamstress and was considered to be quite talented. But it wasn't long before things went very wrong. Charley Ward was arrested for drug trafficking and was sent to Leavenworth Prison. Mollie was left alone to support herself on her meager wages. Even worse, the newspaper reported that she had acquired a drug habit during the time she was with her husband. Desperate for money, she turned to a life of prostitution.

Charley Ward was scheduled to be released in the summer of 1923. Mollie had looked forward to the day when she and Charley could move far away and get a fresh start. But Mollie never got that chance. Instead, just a few short months before Charley was to come home, Mollie was robbed, murdered, and buried in a pauper's grave in the City Cemetery. Life in the red light district was harsh. The sexton's record shows her burial date as March 16, 1923, but doesn't give a specific location. Since the burial expenses were paid for by the county, Mollie may have had a simple wooden marker like the ones shown in the photograph on page 33.

Incidentally, the man who murdered Mollie, Pedro Canno, was convicted and executed in 1926. Charles Ward was allowed to attend Mollie's funeral, accompanied by a prison guard, and then returned to Leavenworth to finish serving his time.

CLAUDE YATES Map: PC 38

CLAUDE LEE YATES had lived in Park City for 43 years when he died on January 17, 1930. He was born in Pine River, Colorado, coming to Park City with his family at the age of two. Claude received his education in Park City's schools, graduating from high school when classes for the older children were still being held in the attic of Lincoln School. Like most other boys in town, Claude went to work in the mines and eventually became the chief electrician at the Silver King Coalition Mine. He married a woman named Larea, and the couple had several children.

Claude survived the plagues and mine disasters that killed many of the town's residents. Although his life certainly wasn't as extraordinary as some of his peers, he represents the majority of those people who lived and died in the camp who lived "normal" lives.

QUARANTINE LAWS FOR 1913
Because there had been so much contagious disease in town, the newspaper published the laws relating to communicable diseases and quarantines. Doctors were by law required to report cases of scarlet fever, diptheria, croup, whooping cough, smallpox, typhoid fever, measles, tuberculosis, cholera, rubella, chicken pox, infantile paralysis (polio), leprosy, plague, or pneumonia. Upon receipt of notification, the house was to be inspected by the local Board of Health, and a placard posted. Anyone exposed to the disease was required, by law, to stay within their homes, and no one was allowed to enter or exit the house, or to violate this quarantine until the infected person was cleared by the rules of the State Board of Health.

GLENWOOD CEMETERY

While City Cemetery pre-dates Glenwood by around five years, Glenwood is by far the more intriguing of the two cemeteries. Nestled in an aspen grove, Glenwood is a five-acre cemetery established in 1885 as an affordable burial place for members of Park City's numerous fraternal orders. Lots sold for $10, and larger plots were $27, which seems very reasonable when one considers that the cost of a pick was $5.00!

As the mines played out and the population decreased, the cemetery was eventually abandoned. Each of the fraternal orders had kept their own records. When these local groups dissolved, some of the records were kept by remaining family members; however, most of the records weren't kept up to date. Glenwood was soon overgrown with weeds, and the aspen groves slowly encroached on the cemetery's boundaries, swallowing up many of its grave sites.

In recent years, Glenwood's grace and dignity has been restored by a group of dedicated volunteers who formed the Glenwood Cemetery Association, relying solely on public donations for its maintenance and preservation. (Donations may be sent to the Glenwood Cemetery Association, P. O. Box 4422, Park City, UT 84060.) They are its rescuers, its caretakers, safeguarding this historical burial ground for future generations. The association only asks that you "please be respectful and reverent at all times."

Take Park Ave. (Hwy. 224) to Empire Ave. Turn west toward the ski lifts. Turn right on Silver King Dr. and go to the end of the road.

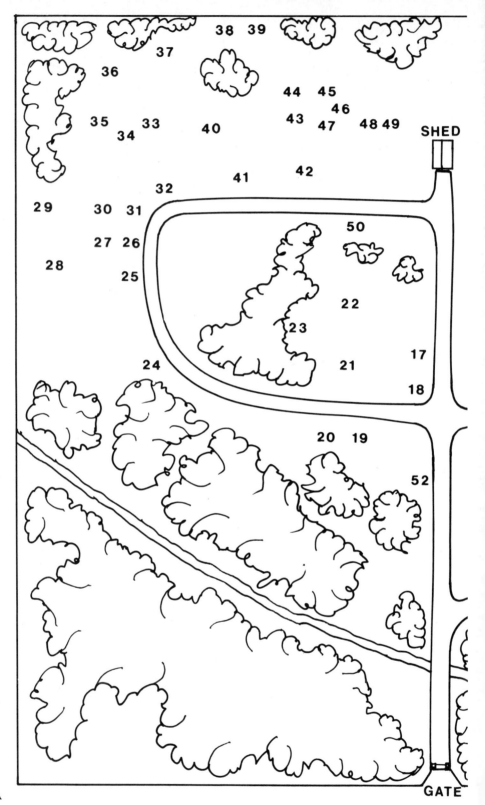

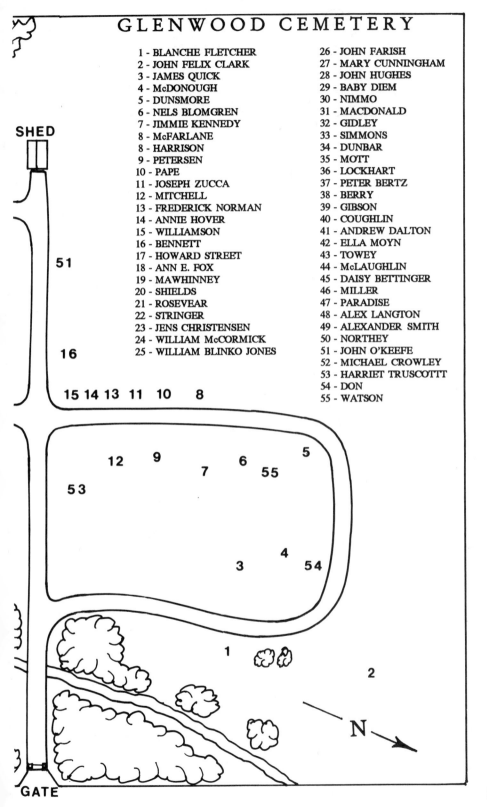

STORIES IN STONE

FRED & CLARISSA BENNETT   Map: GW 16

Cholera claimed the life of six-month-old Fred C. Bennett in August of 1886. His sister, Clarissa, is buried at his side in the same family plot. She died of pneumonia in 1891 at around two years of age. I've decided to include these children in this book, because their father was City Marshal Bill Bennett, one of Park City's most interesting local characters.

William "Bill" Bennett was a poor miner who was unemployed much of the time. He lived with his wife, who was also named Clarissa, and their six children in a tiny, dirt-floored shanty on the outskirts of town.

The story goes that because Bill didn't make enough money mining to keep his children fed, he set off dynamite charges to kill trout in the local streams. One day, however, he under-estimated the blast time and blew off his right arm. The townspeople, quite concerned about what would become of the children, decided Bill should become town marshal. Now, this would have been a strange job for a man who reportedly drank too often and had a bad temper. But the fact was that Bill was a very large man who feared no one, although most everyone was afraid of him. So, the logic in appointing him as town marshal was that no one would dare to challenge him. The very fact that Bennett was marshal was sure to keep some of the rowdy miners in line.

Marshal Bennett gave up drinking and wore his badge proudly. When the town raised enough money to buy him a false arm, complete with sharp, intimidating hook, and gave Bill a fancy six-gun, he became the bane of Park City's lawless. The one-armed marshal of Park City never showed fear, literally hooking criminals and bringing them to justice. That was in 1887.

Marshal Bennett was stead-fast in his work to clean up Park City, pursuing criminals, arresting drunk, boisterous miners and taking them to jail to sober up, and breaking up the fights that frequently broke out in the saloons.

Although it's unknown just how long Bill Bennett served the town as marshal, we do know he was still here in 1893, as the newspaper reported Marshal Bill broke his false arm. But this wasn't a big problem, as he simply removed it and sent it down into Salt Lake City for repairs.

Glenwood Cemetery

William H. Bennett, was a member of the Ancient Order of United Workmen of the Ontario Mine, and it's believed his children are buried in one of the sections of the cemetery set aside for this fraternal order.

MARTHA & EDWARD BERRY   Map: GW 38

A very crude stone marker is all that's left of Martha C. Berry's monument. It looks as if someone has painted her name, birth and death date on a broken piece of the headstone.

Martha was the wife of Edward Berry and the mother of Annie, both of whom lie with her in the family plot. There was little data available about Martha's life. However, historical records indicate that Edward, who was born on January 12, 1862, came to Park City with his brother from New York around 1880 as a single man. He was a blacksmith by trade. Later, the Berry Brothers owned and operated the local blacksmith shop.

Ed loved horse racing, particularly races with horse-drawn carts. During the 1880s, he often raced in his cart against the town's most famous physician, Dr. LeCompte, though there's no record of who actually won!

Life must have been rough for Ed, as both his wife and daughter died within two years of each other. Martha was only 32 when she died in 1894, and little Annie, who died of congestion of the lungs, was six.

Ed W. Berry was the chief of the volunteer fire department, organized in 1881. For 24 years he served in that position. He was finally replaced by his son, W. J. Berry, who was the fire chief for more than 40 years.

STORIES IN STONE

PETER BERTZ   Map: GW 37

On October 20, 1896, Peter Bertz blew his head off with a shotgun. That morning Peter told his wife and six children he was going to hunt chickens. Then he went to a neighbor's house and borrowed a No. 10 magazine shotgun. (These must have been large chickens to require that size of a blast to bring them down!) Mrs. Bertz told the authorities that her husband had been despondent and had often threatened to blow his brains out, so at first it was assumed Peter had committed suicide.

Now, it's true that Peter's body was found at the bottom of a dump, lying back in a reclining position with the shotgun between his feet, barrel pointed at his head. But the coroner, for some unknown reason, decided that it was an accidental death!

DAISY BETTINGER   Map: GW 45

Daisy was the 17-month-old daughter of George and Anna Bettinger, who died during a diptheria epidemic in December of 1892. Deeply distressed over Daisy's death, the grieving parents wrote a note to the local newspaper to thank the people of Park City for their kindness and sympathy during this time of sorrow: "Our heart-felt wish is that each one may find friends as kind when trouble shall cast his brooding shadow over them or theirs."

The headstone is carved white limestone with a delicate lamb resting on top. It would appear that a photograph originally sat in the square above Daisy's name.

Glenwood Cemetery

NELS BLOMGREN   Map: GW 6

Nels Blomgren's monument is etched with the words "At Rest." Nels died at the young age of 33, passing from this world in September of 1894. He was one of the large number of Swedes who migrated to Park City for mining riches in the early 1890s. Nels was active in the Masons and Lodge No. 27 of the A.O.U.W.

It seems that Nels, who was employed by the Daly mine, was mysteriously attacked while down in Salt Lake, where he'd gone with a group of friends to get his naturalization papers. Later, Nels separated from the group for some unknown reason. What's remarkable is that when he was found the next day, he was barely conscious, lying on a pile of pipes behind a plumbing business. His face and clothing were covered with blood, and his speech was slurred. He was taken to City Hall rather than to a hospital, as it was assumed he was drunk. By the time someone decided to take the poor man to the hospital, it was too late. Nels died a short time later of a fractured skull. The case was investigated by the famous Pinkerton Investigation Agency. But detectives were unable to determine whether it was murder or an accident, and the case remained unsolved, in spite of the fact his friends and family were sure it was foul play.

JENS CHRISTIAN CHRISTENSEN   Map: GW 23

Born in 1842 in Denmark, Christian (as he called himself) committed suicide by hanging. The newspaper reported that he had been worried about going insane, so before he did himself in, he sold all of his property and stocks. He was 52 when he died on October 5, 1894. This was just one of the numerous suicides in Park City.

JOHN FELIX CLARK   Map: GW 2

Born December 18, 1899, John had lived his entire life in Park City. He was only 18, a teenager who had recently graduated from high school. John worked at the Judge Smelter, but it wasn't the mines that took his life.

In February of 1918, another diphtheria epidemic hit Park City. Even a big, strapping youth like John Clark wasn't spared from its deadly grip.

John complained of a sore throat, so the doctor prescribed medicine and a special gargle, cautioning the parents to watch carefully for further symptoms which would determine if diphtheria were present. When John didn't get any better, his parents tried to reach the physician by telephone. But he was attending to another patient, so Mr. and Mrs. Clark contacted a second doctor, who didn't believe John had diphtheria and discarded the original doctor's special gargle.

That was a fatal mistake, for as the days passed, it became evident that John's condition was growing worse. So, a third doctor was called for a consultation. John was diagnosed with a full-blown case of diphtheria, and the Clark home was quarantined. Doctor No. 3 tried to round up some anti-toxin for the young man, but there was only a little left in town. Unfortunately, it was too little too late, and John died a short time later.

The controversy raged. Was doctor No. 2 negligent? But things soon calmed down, and fortunately, John's siblings didn't catch diphtheria.

John was the son of Patrick and Minnie Clark. Patrick came to the U. S. from Scotland in the 1890s. When he first arrived in Park City, he worked in the mines. But Patrick Clark ended up running one of the local saloons by 1903. Although John was buried in Glenwood, his parents are buried in Park City Cemetery.

PATRICK COUGHLIN   Map: GW 40

Even as a teenager, Patrick Coughlin was constantly in and out of trouble, and was described by the local newspaper as one of the town's "tough kids." He had been involved in numerous burglaries and petty thefts, and by the time he was 20, Patrick had spent time in jail for allegedly shooting a man. (Coughlin was eventually acquitted of this crime.)

But it was the now-famous "strawberry incident" that brought an end to his short life. It all began when Coughlin and two friends, Fred George and Frank Kennedy, stole some boxes of strawberries and sold them to one of the madams up on the "row." Kennedy was caught, telling the authorities that Coughlin and George were planning a much bigger heist -- holding up a payroll train. When Coughlin got word about Kennedy's confession, he and George high-tailed it out of town on "borrowed" horses. The pair lead several posses from various towns on a wild 200 mile chase. The young fugitives, who started their crime spree with strawberries, ended up shooting and killing two law enforcement officers.

When they were finally caught, Patrick Coughlin was sentenced to death, and his partner, Fred George, received a life sentence. Patrick was only 22 when he was executed by a firing squad in Sage Hollow, about a mile from Randolph. His body was returned to Glenwood Cemetery for burial in the Coughlin family plot in a shady section near the southwest corner.

MICHAEL CROWLEY   Map: GW 52

Michael Crowley was one of the many local men who died on July 15, 1902, in Park City's greatest mining disaster. His gravestone is one of the first monuments you'll see on the left when walking up the main road in Glenwood. The large gravesite was purchased by his widow, Mary, who wanted it to be a special place for her husband. It was originally surrounded by turned wooden posts, now rotting and splintered. Michael lies at rest alone in the plot--apparently Mary moved away from Park City.

MARY CUNNINGHAM   Map: GW 27

Mary Cunningham's tombstone, a cube resting on edge atop an obelisk, is a very unusual design and the only one of its kind in Park City. Mary lived to the ripe old age of 86, undoubtedly some sort of record in the early days of Park City.

Mary and her husband, Thomas, were born in New York. The couple came to Park City in 1876, where, by the time of her death of 1930, she had been a resident for more than 54 years. She was survived by three children.

STORIES IN STONE

ANDREW DALTON   Map: GW 41

Andrew Dalton was born in 1843 in Connary, Ireland. He died of lead poisoning, more commonly called "lead colic," in January of 1895. Dalton, like many other men who worked in the mines of Park City, was a victim of his occupation. By May, 1894, the problem of lead poisoning among men working in the Ontario Mill had become a big concern to Parkites. The newspaper reported that the new yield of silver ore at the Ontario was particularly high in lead content, thus causing the outbreak of illness associated with breathing the dust of the ore-laden rock as it was chipped away in the depths of the earth or crushed in the stamp mills.

BABY DIEM   Map: GW 29

"Baby" Diem was delivered prematurely on October 13, 1901, and lived only one day. Around the turn of the century, the baby's father, John Diem, worked as a harnessmaker for the Consolidated Wagon and Machine Company. John and Mabel Diem eventually became wealthy from their extensive mining interests. John also owned the large Diem Building, which housed such businesses as the local dentist. But like so many other Park City residents who got ahead financially, John and Mabel left Park City. Poor little Baby Diem was left behind...alone in a large, empty plot that was obviously meant to be the final resting place for the entire family.

Typhoid fever was one of many diseases carried through polluted water sources.

Glenwood Cemetery

DON   Map: GW 54

The Dons were among the town's most well-respected families. At the age of 75, William Don was employed as a night watchman at the Daly-Judge Tunnel. One night, the old gentleman was injured in a fall. He took a chill, which developed into bronchitis. A few days later, on June 30, 1914, he died. William was born in Fifeshire, Scotland, in 1839, and came to Park City in 1883. His wife, Annie, lies by his side. Judge James W. Don, the son of William and Annie Don, served as the City Justice. When Judge James Don died in 1932, his coffin was placed atop a fire truck, accompanied by a huge funeral procession which traveled down Main Street to his grave. His wife, Ada Huffman Don, is buried with him.

DUNBAR   Map: GW 34

One of the most unusual headstones in Glenwood Cemetery is the monument for the Dunbar children, William Bruce, age three, and Bessie, age two. Carved out of stone, the tiny diamond-tufted chair is draped with a child's cape and straw hat, and at its base rests a pair of high-button shoes. (Straw hats were very fashionable during warm months and were worn by both boys and men.)

The children's father, William, Sr., was from Nova Scotia, while their mother, Margaret (Maggie) was from Utah. Like so many other Parkites, William was a miner, but it's most likely he was fairly well-to-do, as a monument of this caliber must have been quite expensive. (A similar monument is located in Park City Cemetery next to James Judge.)

Little Bessie succumbed to pneumonia in 1901, and William died of scarlet fever on May 4, 1903. Bessie's name can be seen chiseled onto the side of the stone, while William's name and dates are on the back.

43

STORIES IN STONE

DUNSMORE   Map: GW 5

A dove of peace flies through the pearly gates on Ellen Dunsmore's elegant monument. Ellen was born in 1868 and died in 1908 at the age of 40. There are many Dunsmore family members in this same area, including John Dunsmore, Ellen's husband, and several of her children. Born in 1864, John Dunsmore was an engineer. Both John and Ellen were from Scotland. The Dunsmores lived in the Lake Flat (Deer Valley) on the outskirts of Park City, as the *Park Record* reported in the mid-1890s that their neighbors gave them a surprise party in their home in that area. John outlived Ellen by thirty years.

Their son, James, married a girl named Clara from Midway, Utah, on Dec. 20, 1917. A year later, Clara was dead, one of Park City's victims of the Spanish flu.

In the Fall and Winter of 1918 an influenza epidemic swept around the world, claiming in its destructive path millions of lives. Park City officials, trying to head-off the flu before it struck their town, took as many precautions as possible. With cases of flu in Coalville, Heber, and surrounding towns, all public places were closed, including schools and churches. People were advised to stay home in an effort to keep the viruses from spreading. For once it hit, there was no stopping the killer Spanish Influenza.

In spite of their best efforts, a number of Parkites died, including 25-year-old Clara. James also caught the flu. Although it didn't kill him immediately, he became so weakened that he died a year later at the age of 31. The official cause of death was carcinoma of the glands, although a newspaper article reported that James had never fully recovered from the Spanish flu that had killed his young wife.

JOHN H. FARISH   MAP: GW 26

John Farish was born in Kentucky in 1830 and was 64 at the time of his death in November of 1894. He lived a fascinating life, working as a cowboy in Texas for a while, then moving to California where he drove cattle across the country to market. Farish also did a lot of prospecting in California's Mother Lode, Death Valley, and in the mountains of Nevada.

Glenwood Cemetery

After he heard the news about the silver strikes in Park City, John headed for Utah, arriving in camp in 1874. He worked at the Ontario Mine as a blacksmith for 13 years while searching for silver in the mountains around Park City. According to Farish's obituary, "...he located several valuable groups of claims, among them being the Silver King and West Ontario." Farish was also credited as being the "direct means of discovering" the Woodside Mine. He netted a fortune from these three mines, purchasing interests in other claims and several buildings in town.

In 1894, Farish's health had been weakened by a gunshot wound--although records don't say how or why he was shot--and he died a short time later of pneumonia. The town held a big funeral for Farish, the wealthy prospector who loved children and had no children of his own. His dying wish was that the schools would be closed so that the town's children could attend his memorial service. The whole town complied.

Note that John Farish's obelisk was moved from another location and now sits atop a Chapman grave marker. Most likely, John's headstone was broken from its own base and reattached to the wrong base. Thus, we'll never know exactly where his body lies.

BLANCHE FLETCHER   Map: GW 1

The history of Glenwood Cemetery would be incomplete without the story of Blanche Fletcher, a feisty woman who lived in Park City for more than 93 years. Blanche was born in Park City in 1888, the daughter of Harry and Matilda Wiest. (The Wiests are also buried in Glenwood. Harry, a barber by trade, was a member of the volunteer fire department. In 1910 he died from pneumonia, which he developed after fighting the fire which burned down the Red Maple Hall, a social hall located next to today's Claimjumper Restaurant.)

While Blanche was a student at the old Catholic school, she worked at a local bakery, earning $3.00 a week. But her real forte was playing the piano. She had a love of music, a beautiful voice, and was a talented musician. Blanche was soon snatched up by several Park City theaters to play for the silent films. As a matter of fact, that's how she met her husband, Roy, who was working as a projectionist at the time. In an interview with Blanche shortly before her death, she said that she didn't even like Roy at first, although he was quite handsome. But after a while...well, she married him!

Roy and Blanche continued to make their home in Park City, where Blanche bore five children. Roy worked as a paperhanger and sign painter, and is perhaps best remembered for the beautiful gold-leafing he did on office windows in town.

Roy died in 1966, and Blanche died at the age of 94 in 1982. She had an interesting life, one filled with rich experiences...like the time she was deputized to search a woman prisoner in the town's jail. And there was the night in 1916 when the roof of the Dewey Theater collapsed under the weight of a record snowfall. Blanche was the pianist that night and she, along with 300 people, had left the theater only a few hours before the would-be disaster. There were also the countless dances, weddings, and funerals at which she had provided the music, including the funeral of D.L.H. DeGrover (see his story). Around 1979, she appeared in a movie which was filmed in Park City, riding a float through town dressed as the Snow Queen! At the age of 79, Blanche became a model, posing in the latest ski fashions for ski journals for the Park City Ski Resort.

Yes, Blanche did it all. Retaining her sharp wit until the time of her death, Blanche liked to joke about herself, saying that "The old gray mare ain't what she used to be." But, she would add, she was still here, and she was "gonna stay," too. And stay she has--at peace in her beloved Park City with her husband, Roy.

ANN E. FOX   Map: GW 18

On the corner near the Street grave lies Ann E. Fox, wife of Francis S. Fox. Ann, who was one of Park City's first music teachers, died in March of 1889.

JOHN S. GIBSON   Map: GW 39

John S. Gibson was born in Salt Lake City in 1866 and moved to Park City around 1877 to work as a teamster. Most likely, he hauled freight for the mines, but eventually wound up working in the Ontario Mine.

Glenwood Cemetery

In early 1899, John Gibson had a streak of bad luck. First, he was laid off of his job in the Ontario Mine. Then his mother died. Things started to look up when he began working again, but another blow came on June 23, 1899 when his son, Alvin, died from spinal meningitis. John and his wife, Annie, buried Alvin near their daughter, Jennet, who had died in 1892 at the age of two.

Life is full of ironies, however, and John's return to work was one of them. Four days after John buried his son, he was killed at the Ontario No. 3 mine shaft while loading waste-filled ore cars on the cage. No one knew what caused the accident, but before the cars were hoisted to the surface, the cage suddenly shifted. John was crushed between the cage and the wall plates and died almost immediately.

Annie, John's widow, was left behind to raise their two small children. Since John had been out of work, his membership had lapsed in the A.O.U.W. Had it been reactivated in time, the organization would have helped the widow with burial expenses and insurance. Since the couple had fallen on hard times, some of their friends or family undoubtedly came to the financial aid of the widow.

What does the pile of bricks represent? Is this a memorial to all of the Gibson family members? It would appear that John S. Gibson was buried with a simple headstone in 1899 and that this unique monument was added sometime later. This touching inscription graces the monument:

> *Like the dove to the ark*
> *Thou hast flown to thy rest,*
> *From the wild sea of strife,*
> *To the home of the blest.*

STORIES IN STONE

ANNIE & WILLIAM GIDLEY   Map: GW 32

Annie Gidley died at the age of 39. The cause of death is listed as peritonitis (inflammation of the lining of the abdominal cavity). She left behind an infant, Robert, and a husband, William, who was the sexton of both Glenwood and Park City Cemeteries. It was William's job to dig the graves, act as the caretaker, and keep the cemetery records. On August 26, 1903, he dug a grave for his dear wife, Annie.

William suffered another blow a year later when two-year-old Robert died of scarlet fever, the same illness which had taken the life of Gidley's three-year-old-son, Frederick, in 1893. Frederick and Robert lie beside their mother in this family plot.

Annie was born in Salt Lake City on February 14, 1864. Like most of the women in Park City, Annie's role was that of wife and mother. She was active in local organizations, like the Ladies Aide Society of the Methodist Episcopal Church.

William Gidley was undoubtedly one of the town's more interesting characters. When an early prohibition came to Utah in 1917, it was Gidley who rang the "grave digger's bell" at midnight to announce the end of liquor consumption in Park City...undoubtedly a death-knell for the town's saloons. Because William was deaf in one ear, a hearing horn dangled from his neck. Ironically, when William Gidley died, his name wasn't even entered in the cemetery records. He lived until August 1, 1917, outliving his wife by 14 years.

HARRY HARRISON   Map: GW 8

Harry Harrison died of Bright's Disease in 1904. Bright's Disease wasn't terribly common, although there were numerous people who died of this kidney disease in Park City. It was believed that Bright's was caused by over-eating rich foods, drinking coffee or alcohol, or using tobacco, all of which contributed to wearing out the kidneys. Of course, this couldn't have been the case in Harry's death, as he was only nine years old. Young Harry is buried next to his sister and brother, who both died in February of

1903 (a year before his death) during a scarlet fever epidemic. Cherry McFarlane, his mother, is buried next to him. John McFarlane was her second husband (see McFarlane's story).

ANNIE HOVER   Map: GW 14

Annie* and her husband, J. H. Hover, lived in a small house in Empire Canyon on top of the old joisting works. One day as Mr. Hover prepared to leave for work, he noticed Annie was feeling ill and depressed. After he had gone, Mrs. Hover began having convulsions and called to a neighbor's child to get help. Mr. Hover had only been at work for a few minutes when he was summoned home and found his dying wife. Annie died five minutes after her husband returned home, in spite of the neighbor's efforts to revive her with a concoction of coffee and lemon juice.

According to Mr. Hover, Annie had been depressed because of some bad news she had received from the doctor--that she probably wouldn't be able to have children. He also told the newspaper that much of her distress was because of the fact that he had "too much animal magnetism and was, by intercourse, slowly sapping her life away." He added that this had "all preyed on her mind." Dr. Gregor testified that her symptoms suggested she had taken strychnine, although no stomach analysis was done.

Annie's funeral was held at the Methodist Church, and she was buried at Glenwood. Although the cemetery records show the location of her grave, there's no headstone. Was it one of those wooden markers which rotted into oblivion decades ago? Or was it broken into pieces and removed? Today, a cluster of small trees grows in the spot where Annie is buried.

We know little about Annie, except that she was born in Scotland. Annie committed suicide on August 17, 1892.

(*While Glenwood Cemetery records list her as "Annie" W. Hover, the newspaper calls her "Jennie" Hover.)

REXALL OLIVE OIL EMULSION WAS RECOMMENDED AS THE BEST REMEDY FOR PEOPLE WHO WERE RUN-DOWN, TIRED, OR NERVOUS...NO MATTER WHAT THE CAUSE!

STORIES IN STONE

JOHN HUGHES   Map: GW 28

John A. Hughes lies buried in Glenwood Cemetery, but his headstone has disappeared. Perhaps you can find his elusive monument, which is most likely hidden among the aspen trees. Because John's story was so interesting, I've decided to include it in this little book.

John Hughes was from Cornwall, England. The date of his birth is unknown, although he was considered "elderly" by the time of his death in 1892. "Johnny" Hughes was one of the very first prospectors in what is now Park City. He and a man named McHenry were partners in the discovery of the McHenry Mine around 1872, one of the first ore strikes in the area. In fact, the first mining camp in Park City was built around a high mountain lake near the McHenry Mine.

Hughes lived in Park City for the next 20 years. He was one of the old breed of prospectors, continuing to roam the mountains and streams in search of the next big strike. Then in November of 1892, his body was discovered lying face up on the old McHenry Mine dump. Because he'd been dead for quite a few days, the cause of his death was never determined--it may have been exposure or, more likely, it was murder. Officially, it was ruled heart failure. Hughes was the first of Park City's old-time prospectors to die, and with his passing came the beginning of the end of an era.

WILLIAM B. JONES   Map: GW 25

William Blinko Jones was born in London, England, in 1841 and died on January 1, 1900. His headstone, resembing stacked logs, is an interesting tribute to his occupation and affiliation with the Woodmen of the World organization. William died of pulmonary tuberculosis, leaving behind his wife, Elizabeth Jones.

Glenwood Cemetery

JIMMIE T. KENNEDY   Map: GW 7

James "Jimmie" Kennedy was a casualty of the mines, killed in one of the frequent accidents that occurred in Park City. On July 30, 1896, Jimmie was working in the No. 5 shaft of the Ontario when a huge slab of rock overhead gave way, crushing him beneath its weight. Jimmie, who was 28, had married Julia Canty six months earlier.

These mining accidents were mourned by the entire town, as it reminded them of the constant dangers which their husbands, sons, and friends experienced each time they entered the depths of the mountains. Jimmie Kennedy had grown up in Park City and had been known by everyone in the community. He was a member of the Miners' Union and the A.O.U.W. (Ancient Order of United Workmen of the Ontario Mine). The mine was shut down so his friends and co-workers could attend the services in the Catholic Church.

ALEX LANGTON   Map: GW 48

Alex Langton was murdered on September 12, 1890 by W. J. Moss, an engineer at the Ontario Mine. Moss shot Langton after an argument in Moxby and Nichols' Capital Saloon. Alex Langton had been a private investigator for an eastern agency (probably Pinkerton), while living in Colorado before moving to Park City. He had told his friends that he had seen several men whom he had previously investigated. Alex feared that they were planning to get even with him for the role he played in the prosecution of one of their partners in Colorado. So, when he was murdered, authorities believed that Moss was carrying out a vendetta against Langton. W. J. Moss was taken to Salt Lake and tried for murder, most likely facing a firing squad.

Alex Langton was unmarried and 40 years old at the time of his death. He was a member of the Knights of Pythias and is listed in the Glenwood records; however, his headstone is among the many missing monuments, as a thorough search in this section was made, and Langton's marker could not be found. I've marked the map with the approximate location where Alex Langton lies at rest.

LOCKHART   Map: GW 36

This granite monument is very spartan, simply listing the names of each person buried in the Lockhart plot. Oliver C. and Walter Scott Lockhart were both respected citizens of Park City throughout their lives. Oliver was the manager of the Utah Power and Light Company, a town councilman, a member of the school board, and he served on the fire and water committees. Walter Lockhart was the Justice of the Peace in 1899 and owned one of the local mercantile stores. Oliver was born in 1856 and died in 1933, and Walter was born in 1853 and died in 1907.

This headstone was probably erected much later, as the graves are scattered around the monument. Incidentally, the children--Frank and Infant--were Oliver and Mary's children. Mary died of septic peritonitis when she was only 38. Alice may have been Oliver's second wife.

MACDONALD   Map: GW 31

Daniel MacDonald was born in Pictau County, Nova Scotia in 1843 and died in 1891. Although cemetery records state he died of congestion of the lungs, there was apparently some question as to his cause of death, as a coroner's inquest was held in Salt Lake City. Daniel's daughter, Edith Olive, lies by his side with a touching epitaph carved into her monument, which reads "Darling Pet," a reminder of the pain these families suffered when losing a child.

Glenwood Cemetery

MAWHINNEY   Map: GW 19

Another family prominent in early Park City were the Mawhinneys. Ellen Sloan Mawhinney bore 11 children, but by 1910 only six were still living. Robert, Ellen's husband, was an engineer at the Marsac Mill of the Ontario Company. The couple came from Ireland in 1875 and to Park City in 1877, where Robert was fondly known throughout the camp as "Bob."

Tragedy struck over and over for the Mawhinneys. An infant son, John, died at birth in 1880. Then four-year-old Agnes died 20 days later. Another daughter, Rachael, died in 1886. All of these children had been buried in the Park City Cemetery. However, when 15-year-old Mary Mawhinney died of dropsy in 1889, Bob and Ellen purchased a large plot at the newly opened Glenwood Cemetery. Bob had been a member of the Odd Fellows Lodge for more than 25 years, so his plot is situated in that portion of the cemetery. John, Agnes, and Rachael's bodies were exhumed and moved to Glenwood in 1889.

The Marsac Mill where Bob worked was on the east end of town, and the family lived a few blocks away. When the fire of 1898 swept through Park City leaving most of the town in ashes, the Mawhinneys lost their home and everything they owned. But they were a hardy lot, deciding to rebuild on the same spot.

Then, shortly after they'd moved into their new house in 1899, Bob died of pneumonia, the sickness that claimed more lives in Park City than any epidemic or disease. He was buried with his four children. Two years later, another child, Robert, Jr., died of spinal meningitis. Losing her husband and then his name-sake must have devastated poor Ellen. In spite of her losses, Ellen remained in the town that had been so cruel to her until her death in 1924. Ellen lies with her family at Glenwood.

WILLIAM McCORMICK   Map: GW 24

William McCormick was 48 years old when he met with a violent death. While on a visit to Salt Lake City in January of 1881, he was stabbed, dying of his wounds in a Salt Lake City hospital a short time later. Was it a knife fight or foul play? The records only state that he was "cut with a knife," so we'll never know the answer. McCormick's body was first interred in the Park City Cemetery. But sometime after 1885 when Glenwood Cemetery was opened, his remains were moved to the new cemetery, where he lies in the section reserved for the Ancient Free and Accepted Masons, which was chartered in Park City in 1880.

BARTLY & MINNIE McDONOUGH   Map: GW 4

Bartly McDonough left his native Ireland in 1886 and came to America to work in the mines of Park City. He met and married Minnie in 1890. The young couple had seven children, lots of mouths to feed on Bartly's wages working in the mines. However, he prospered at his work. Bartly became active in city politics, serving on the City Council and the Board of the Directors for the Miner's Hospital in 1905. The author was also told that Bartly was Park City's sheriff for a number of years.

Bartly McDonough was born August 25, 1856, and died in 1910 of the "dread disease," miner's consumption. Minnie lived until 1940, dying of a heart attack at the age of 79.

Bartly belonged to at least two secret orders, as can be seen by the carvings on his marble headstone. The insignia on the right symbolized the A.O.U.W. (Ancient Order of United Workmen), which was a fraternal organization of miners at the Ontario Mine. It's unknown what the skull and cross bones represented.

Diptheria was one of the most frequent causes of childhood death in the world until the 1930s, when a vaccine was discovered.

Glenwood Cemetery

WILLIAM & JOHNNIE McLAUGHLIN   Map: GW 44

William McLaughlin was one of Park City's many war veterans. Born in New York in 1846, William was a private in the Union Army. He was about 17 when he fought for the North in the Civil War. Later, he married, raising his family in Park City and working in the mines. He died in 1900 of miner's consumption.

Silicosis, or "miner's con," as it was frequently called, was a by-product of hard-rock mining. Quartz dust became airborne during drilling and stamping the ore. Microscopic particles lodged in the miner's lungs, cutting into the tissue. Death from miner's con was so frequent in Park City that a hospital was eventually founded to care for the victims of this painful ailment. The Western Federation of Miners Local No. 144 initiated the construction of the hospital around the turn of the century. Prior to this time, miners dying of the con were cared for in the Judge Memorial Hospital in Salt Lake City, which had been built by Mary Judge, widow of mining magnate John Judge, after her husband's death in 1892 from miner's con. Miner's Hospital in Park City was finally opened in 1904.

William's son, Johnnie, is buried in the same plot. Perhaps it was because Johnnie watched his father's slow, painful death from the con that he decided to find a job outside the mines. Johnnie was the stagehand at the Dewey Theater on Main Street. Some of the country's finest entertainers performed at the Dewey, and it was a job he loved. The irony is that the mines still claimed Johnnie's life when he was only 21.

Like the rest of the town, Johnnie awoke in the early morning hours of July 15, 1902, to the clanging of the warning bell that spelled disaster in the mines. Everyone rushed to the scene to see if they could help. Johnnie and several other men were among the first to take the first rescue cage into the bowels of the earth. On their return trip to the surface, they brought up only dead bodies. Refusing to give up, the young men took the cage down for a second time. Later, rescue teams found Johnnie and his fellow heroes. But it was too late. They had been overcome by poisonous fumes. Johnnie gasped his final breath upon reaching the surface. All of the heroes died that day.

(Note: There is another Wm. McLaughlin buried near Bertz & Lockhart. This William McLaughlin was one of 12 young men from Park City to serve in the Spanish-American War. The boys were inducted into the Army on April 30, 1898. William survived the war, returning to Park City. It's believed he worked as a barber.)

HANNAH & WILLIAM MILLER   Map: GW 46

William Miller was born in Scotland and was one of the miners who managed to make a great deal of money. In 1897, we know that Miller was a delegate for the Western Federation of Miners. Besides his association with the mines, Miller was a well-known businessman. He owned the old Park City Hotel, which unfortunately burned to the ground in July of 1911. The *Park Record* reported in July of 1912 that "Bill" Miller was "rustling hard to get the capital to do the rebuilding." Miller served as the county assessor for a while and was a partner in one of the town's numerous saloon's with a man named Francis Kargeeg. But Miller was best known as the leader of the Park City Brass Band.

Music was important to the people of Park City, as evidenced by its many local bands. In 1904, the Park City Brass Band finally got snappy new uniforms--brilliant green trimmed with gold. They played at funerals, dances, and sporting events, such as the Park City baseball team's games. Each New Year's Eve, the town's bands would gather together with members of the various lodges and the town's most "respectable" men, and parade through the streets of the city. Moving from house to house, they'd stop to feast and entertain. (This is quite reminiscent of an old Scottish New Year's custom and may have originated with the large number of Scots living in Park City.)

Miller headed the Park City Brass Band for many years, dying in the winter of 1920 at the age of 56. Sadly, we know little about his wife,

Glenwood Cemetery

Hannah, other than the fact that she, too, was born in Scotland and that she gave birth to a still-born son, William, Jr., in 1893. Hannah died a year later at the age of 29 and was buried beside the infant. William outlived her by nearly 27 years.

JOHN McFARLANE   MAP: GW 8

Born in Scotland in 1834, John McFarlane was employed at the Ontario Mine in spite of the fact he was 63 years old. On February 4, 1893, a cave-in of "monster proportions" took his life while he was working on a stope below the 600-foot level. John was instantly buried by tons of waste rock and earth.

John and his wife, Cherry, had come to Park City from Nevada two years earlier. He wasn't a member of any of the societies and had no insurance. Upon his death, one of the mine's owners, R. C. Chambers, apparently paid for John's cemetery plot and headstone, as John's widow was destitute. John McFarlane's grave is near Harry Harrison, who was his step-son.

ROBERT MITCHELL   Map: GW 12

The Mitchell family lived in a small whip-sawed board house along the dirt road just below Ontario School (not far from the Ontario Mine). Robert, the son of John and Kate Mitchell, was born in Butte, Montana on May 2, 1899. There were very few automobiles in Park City until the Model T Fords became the popular mode of transportation after 1909. Sadly, Robert died in May, 1920 in an auto accident at the age of 21.

Robert's father, J. P. Mitchell, lies to his immediate right. J. P. Mitchell's monument is topped with a carved stone log, and a symbol of the Woodmen of the World inside Heaven's open gates is etched on the front. The elder Mitchell was born in Ireland and died in Park City of heart trouble at the age of 56. Another Mitchell son, Sylvester, died in 1929 while serving in the U. S. Navy. He is buried to his father's right.

CLYDE LEROY MOTT
Map: GW 35

Clyde Leroy Mott, the infant son of Dow and Lucretia Mott, died of cerebral meningitis in February of 1894. He was one of six children. The Mott family came to Park City from Iowa in the 1870s. Other family members lie in the family plot. Little Clyde's father, Dow, died in 1902 of miner's consumption at the age of 66.

This monument is particularly touching, with its fallen dove and inscription which reads:

> "Budded on Earth to
> Bloom in Heaven."

ELLA MOYN
Map: GW 42

Ella Moyn was born in 1866 in Denver, Colorado, when the mining boom in that area was still in its early stages. From there, she lived at Fort Sill in the Indian Territory, coming to Park City before 1880 to live with her uncle, John Huey, and her aunt. When Ella was only 23, she suffered an "inflammation of one of the veins in an extremity." The newspaper reported that although she was improving, a clot broke loose and killed her. She died in 1889. Ella never had a chance to marry.

JOHN NIMMO
Map: GW 30

Like so many other Parkites, John Nimmo and his wife, Maggie (Margaret) emigrated from Scotland. John worked as a timberman in the quartz mill, but by 1896, he actually owned mining interests in another mining district. However, that mine was shut down because of water in the shaft.

John Nimmo played a controversial role in the 1902 mine explosion which claimed 34 men's lives. Nimmo, who was Foreman of the Daly West Mine, refused to allow the cage to be lowered into the shaft in order to save several men's lives. Nimmo feared that the poisonous gases would overcome the rescuers, and that more lives would be needlessly lost. When the crowd finally pressured him into allowing several men to descend into the mine shaft, one of the injured miners was found, barely breathing. He died a short time after he was brought to the surface, and the angry miners blamed Nimmo for his death. Had they been allowed to go into the hole sooner, they argued, the man's life could have been saved.

The debate raged for weeks. The newspaper tried to soothe the town's concerns by assuring everyone that Nimmo was only trying to save lives by his actions. Things must have worked out for John, because he stayed in Park City until he died in 1911 of heart problems.

Also buried within the same plot are his wife, Margaret, who lived to the age of 71, and an infant son, John Jr., who died of bronchitis in 1892. Note that there is a missing headstone between the parents' headstone and John Jr.'s marker, an indication that there is another child buried with the family.

FREDERICK NORMAN
Map: GW 13

Frederick Norman's monument is particularly touching because of the inscription at the bottom. It reads: *"'Tis a little grave, but oh have care, for world wide hopes are buried there. How much of light, how much of joy, is buried with our darling boy...rest in peace thou gentle spirit."*

STORIES IN STONE

Eight-year-old Frederick died of scarlet fever on July 4 while the town celebrated the nation's 114th birthday with a parade. No other family members are buried with little Frederick, so it must be assumed the disheartened parents left the city.

DAVID & JOSEPH NORTHEY   Map: GW 50

David and Joseph Northey were two brothers who died almost exactly a month apart--David, age 21, died of typhoid fever, while 19-year-old Joseph died of another frequent killer, cholera. Both of these diseases were constant threats to the citizens of Park City, and it's remarkable that two seemingly healthy young men were taken in their prime with no other signs of illness leading up to their deaths.

These brothers were born in Cornwall, England and came to Park City to mine. Cornishmen were considered among the world's best miners. Together with the Irish, the Cornish made up the bulk of the men who worked within the mines. And with their skills they brought their superstitions--like the legends of the Tommy Knockers, tiny ghosts of dead miners who haunted the tunnels and passageways deep within the earth.

This siamese headstone is in the Independent Order of Oddfellows section.

MERITAL WHITE LINAMENT WAS USED AS A PLASTER FOR SORE THROATS, COLD OF THE LUNGS, CROUP, AND PAINS IN THE CHEST. JUST SATURATE A PIECE OF FLANNEL WITH THE LINAMENT AND APPLY TO THE CHEST.

Glenwood Cemetery

JOHN O'KEEFE   Map: GW 51

Though we don't know the details of the accident, John O'Keefe met his end in a train accident which occurred at Ogden, Utah. Coupling accidents were common back in the days before safety equipment, and train crewmen were frequently crushed between the cars. John, a native of Park City, was 34 when he died. His parents, Thomas and Ellen O'Keefe, are also buried in Glenwood. John was born on August 13, 1867, and died exactly 34 years later on August 13, 1901.

PAPE   Map: GW 10

Jack Pape was the saloon keeper who ran "The Grizzly," one of the town's most popular saloons. Three of his sons are buried in this plot. Two-year-old Bradford died in 1880, a year when typhoid and diptheria epidemics claimed many lives. Originally, the child was buried in Park City Cemetery. Five years later, Jack purchased a family plot in the newly opened Glenwood Cemetery when yet another son, James, was still-born. Bradford's remains were moved and re-buried with his infant brother and the monument was erected for the boys. Two years later, Alfred was buried with his brothers in the same plot and his name was engraved on the back of the stone.

Jack Pape, one of the camp's earliest saloon keepers, was originally from England. In 1883 Jack placed an advertisement in the newspaper, boasting that the Grizzly Saloon carried "none but the choicest brands of liquors, wines, and cigars." Maybe it was the fact that prohibition came early to Park City and put the Grizzly out of business...or maybe it was the great fire of 1898 that wiped him out. We'll never know for sure what made Jack and his wife, Nevada, decide to leave town.

Advertisement from the *Park Record* ... *Prickly Ash Bitters*. *"The majority of the ills of the human body arise from a derangement of the Liver, affecting both the stomach and bowels. In order to affect a cure, it is necessary to remove the cause. Irregular and sluggish action of the Bowels, Headache, Sickness of the Stomach, Pain in the Back and Loins, etc., indicate that the Liver is at fault, and that nature requires assistance to enable this organ to throw off impurities. Prickly Ash Bitters are compounded for this purpose...a safe cure for Dyspepsia, Constipation, Diseased Kidneys, Blood Purifier..."*

STORIES IN STONE

LEWIS PARADISE   Map: GW 47

Lewis Paradise was involved in the love triangle and murder that shocked Park City in April of 1892. Lewis was walking with Hope Fuelling when she was shot by Patrick Milton Trotman. Hope was only 17, and Lewis was 21 at the time of the crime. (See the Hope Fuelling story under Park City Cemetery.)

A few days after the murder/suicide, the local newspaper reported that Lewis Paradise had been involved in another incident. He was arrested for assaulting a madam named Nellie Clark up on "the row." While in an angry rage, Lewis shot two bullets into the floor and then held a 41-caliber Colt pistol to Nellie's ample breast. Fortunately for the woman, when he pulled the trigger the gun misfired and she escaped unharmed. Had he been drinking in an attempt to forget the horrible events that left poor Hope Fuelling dead? We'll never know what motivated the young man.

We do know that he remained in Park City until his death in 1933. It's believed that Lewis had a job at Frankel's store on Main Street. He lived with his parents on the outskirts of Park City below the railroad station. The son of a respected citizen named John Paradise (Knights of Pythias), Lewis H. Paradise lies in a grave that has sunk several feet into the ground.

Other Paradise family members are in nearby plots, including Lewis' brother, an infant who was stillborn in 1890, and John Paradise, probably Lewis' father, who died in 1891 of spinal meningitis. Edward was only 16 when he died of typhoid fever, and J. Edwin, another brother, died a year before Lewis in 1932. It's believed the family came to Park City from Canada sometime around 1890.

Glenwood Cemetery

RAY PETERSEN
Map: GW 9

Ray D. Petersen grew up in Park City, graduating from high school about 1916. The sagging local economy had improved since the war began in Europe in 1914 and silver prices began to rise again. Park City teenagers hung out at the Dewey Theater or, later, at the Orpheum, to see their favorite Fatty Arbuckle or Charlie Chaplin moving picture. Summer evenings, boys and girls met at one of the ice cream parlors, like the one that opened in 1917 in the Hurlbut Building on Main Street.

But life changed dramatically for Ray Petersen on May 25, 1917, when all the local boys were required to register for the draft. The war was raging in Europe, and it must have seemed like a far-off and exotic place to a boy who had grown up in the confines of a mining town in the Wasatch Mountains. Nevertheless, Ray, together with 108 other young men from Park City, did his duty and registered. It wasn't long before the first call took 25 boys, including Ray, to the warfront. When the war had ended, most of Park City's young men came home. But not Ray. He was one of six Parkites who lost their lives in the "Great War." He's buried beside his ten-year-old sister, Eva, who died of scarlet fever.

JAMES QUICK
Map: GW 3

Looking like a scroll tacked onto a chunk of stone, the headstone of James Quick is an unusual monument. James, who was born in England, is one of the numerous Civil War veterans, having served as a Private in the Union Army when he was still a young boy. His wife, Eliza L. Kimball, was most likely the daughter of one of the Kimball Brothers of the Kimball Brothers Stage Line. The 1880 Census records show James Quick as a 28-year-old bachelor, so he met and married Eliza sometime after that time.

STORIES IN STONE

ROSEVEAR   Map: GW 21

Edward was a member of the large Rosevear family. The senior family members, William, Joseph, Elizabeth, and Annie, were born in Cornwall, England, but immigrated to Clearfeet, Pennsylvania, before moving to Park City during the 1890s.

In the 1900 census, William listed his occupation as a timberman, which means that he cut the trees for use in the mines. But by 1903, William had left the hard life of timbering and had opened a drug store, where his son, Edward, worked as a drug clerk.

Although William hadn't worked inside the mines for at least a decade, he died of miner's consumption around 1908, most likely the result of dust particles lodged in his lungs during the time he worked in the mines of Cornwall. His son, Edward J. Rosevear, who is buried in this grave, died in 1905 at the age of 27 of a heart problem.

SHIELDS   Map: GW 20

John Shields was born in Ireland in 1846 and came to Park City in the 1870s. The brothers John and Charles Shields operated a mercantile and grocery store in town which was co-owned with Julius Frankel, a well-known businessman in town. Having lost one son to Park City's icy winters, John's wife, Mary, wanted the boys to live in a safer environment. So, Mary took two of their sons to attend a private school at the Osage Mission in Kansas. Later, in 1891 one of the older boys attended school in Salt Lake City, but was very ill with diphtheria.

In 1895 John Shields played a role in a famous gun fight when he saved the life of Peter Clark. Peter Clark and Henry Nugent had been drinking and gambling at Riley and Towey's gambling hall. The men began to argue, and Clark shot Nugent, who in turn drew a .44 revolver and shot Clark from inside his coat. Clark ran bleeding from the saloon and was found in the street by John Shields, who tied a cord around his arm to stop the bleeding. Thanks to John Shields, Clark survived. However, Nugent died, and Clark stood trial, most likely facing a firing squad.

John Shields' business had been successful, and he was a pillar of the community, serving as mayor from 1886 to 1888. But something went wrong in his later years. On January 31, 1913, he was found dead, lying with a pistol in his hand. John committed suicide at the age of 70. We do know that Mr. Frankel had spun off a successful business in 1907 which competed with Shields Brothers. Charles Shields (John's brother) and his family moved down into the Salt Lake Valley. (Incidentally, Charles Shields' wife organized the first chapter of the Eastern Star in Park City in 1909). Did John kill himself because of business difficulties? Or was it his health?

John Shields' funeral was held at the Catholic Church with so many Parkites in attendance, hundreds of people had to stand outside during the service. Mary Shields remained in Park City, working as a nurse until the 1930s. She was also listed in city records as the secretary/treasurer of Shields Grocery Company, so it's likely that one of the Shields' older sons took over the business after his father's death in 1913. Shields Grocery was located at 735 Park Avenue. Mary lies buried by her husband's side with several of her children.

SAMUEL SIMMONS   Map: GW 33

Samuel Simmons died in one of the most gruesome accidents in Park City's history. On May 16 Simmons and two other men were working in the 1400-foot level of the Anchor Shaft. It was time for lunch, so they entered the cage and rang the bell to be pulled up. Suddenly, something malfunctioned and the cage crashed into the side wall of the shaft, spitting the three men off. Miraculously, one man landed on a small wooden platform and survived. But Sam Simmons and Frank Woolsey fell to the bottom of the shaft. Little was left of either man, their limbs torn from their bodies as they hit the sides of the mine shaft. Sam's funeral was held at the Park City Opera House. Frank's remains were taken to Murray for burial.

Sam Simmons had come to work in Utah's mines from Cornwall, England, when he was a very young man. According to the newspaper, his wife, Rebecca, and child were still in England at the time of his death. Rebecca must have come to Park City when she received the terrible news, staying in town with her brother. Eighteen months later, Park City's harsh wilderness environment claimed her life. Rebecca died of "paralysis bulba" (most likely a form of polio). Just what happened to their child is unknown, but Sam and Rebecca lie together in Glenwood Cemetery.

A. M. B. SMITH   Map: GW 49

One of the town's original residents, Smith was born in Iowa on December 16, 1842, and came to Park City in 1876. He was an active member of the Knights of Pythias and the Ancient Order of United Workmen, two of the numerous fraternal organizations in Park City. Smith spearheaded an effort to purchase land for a cemetery in which members of the local "societies" and their families could be buried--a sort of private cemetery separate from Mr. Snyder's pasture. The new cemetery was named "Glenwood." This project had only recently been completed when Alexander Smith died of rheumatism of the heart at the age of 43.

Alexander Smith owned a livery and feed stable. He was a great horseracing enthusiast and was at least in part responsible for building a straight-line race track in Deer Valley in the 1880s. On the day of the very first race, Smith placed a heavy bet on his own horse, which was running against Colonel Wall's grey stallion. Unfortunately for Smith, the other horse won.

Alexander Smith was so highly regarded and loved by his fellow Parkites that the whole town turned out for his funeral procession. All of the local businesses closed down, and virtually every vehicle and horse in town was part of the march to the grave site. Two local bands accompanied the mourners to the new Glenwood Cemetery where Smith was buried. He never dreamed he would be Glenwood's first occupant.

HOWARD STREET   Map: GW 17

A small weed-filled wooden box is all that's left of Howard Street's monument. Most likely, there was a wooden cross or plank above the child's head at one time which bore his name and dates. Unfortunately, wood doesn't survive the elements, as you can see from the rotting turned-posts at each corner and planks surrounding the tiny enclosure.

Howard was the two-month-old son of Charles E. and Agnes Street. Charles Street played a significant role in Park City's heritage. In fact, the Street family dates back to the camp's very early beginnings.

When he was 15, "Charley" helped his family drive a herd of cattle from Montana to the Park City area in 1874. His father, John, bought four lots in the center of the tiny town, clearing the aspen trees and building what was then the fifth house in Park City. John Street bought the local meat market, as well as the slaughter house located on the lower end of town.

The Street family was also known for providing wood for the Marsac Mill in Park City. They cut and cleared wood from the local hillsides and hauled it into town for use in the mills and mines. Besides his work in the family businesses, Charles Street was the secretary of the Jupiter Mining Co.

In 1947, when Charles Street was 88 years old, he wrote a history of Park City based on his memories, which was used as the basis of a centennial history written for Summit County.

THOMAS STRINGER   Map: GW 22

Born September 12, 1856 in Wales, Thomas Stringer immigrated to America with his family in 1873. When he first came to Park City, he was employed in one of the mine smelters. Later, he operated an assay office in town. He met and married Matilda and raised his family in Park City. Thomas was also involved in local politics, serving on the school board for a number of years. He was the Grand Master of Park City's Oddfellows in 1906 and 1907.

He was also a member of the Woodmen of the World, as can be seen on his massive tombstone. Stringer succumbed to an illness in 1911.

Note all the other family members buried around Thomas...with one striking exception. His wife, Matilda, who outlived Thomas by nearly 18 years, is buried in the Park City Cemetery.

JAMES TOWEY   Map: GW 43

Thirty-two-year-old James Towey died on April 5, 1894, at Holy Cross Hospital in Salt Lake City after a long battle with tuberculosis. Tuberculosis, commonly called consumption at this time, was a fatal disease which killed millions of people each year until a cure was finally discovered shortly after the turn of the century. James' brother, Thomas, who lies in the same family plot, fell to his death in the Ontario mine shaft No. 2 on March 11, 1894.

The Towey family came from County Mayo, Ireland. While many of the Towey men were miners, at least one brother was a partner in Riley and Towey's Gambling Hall in the mid-1890s. Frank Towey, who worked as chairman of the Miner's Union Day celebration, is buried with his wife, Catherine and son, Michael.

HARRIET J. TRUSCOTT   Map: GW 53

Nineteenth century women wore long, full skirts, in which they performed their daily chores. This often proved to be hazardous as can be seen in the death of Harriet Truscott.

Though she knew it was dangerous, Harriet often used coal oil to light the fire in her stove when she was in a hurry to get supper on the table. One Sunday afternoon as Harriet began to prepare dinner, the oil can exploded, spewing the burning oil everywhere. Her dress caught fire, and the poor woman ran into the yard, screaming. Several passers-by managed to extinguish her burning clothing. However, it was too late. Harriet's burns were extensive. While the house burned to the ground, Harriet was taken to a neighbor's house, where she died three days later. She must have been too serious to move down into Salt Lake.

Harriet was born in Cornwall, England. Her husband, William, was at work in the Daly Mine the day of the accident. Harriet, who was 56 years old, was an active member of the Ladies Aid Society of the local Methodist Church.

P. B. WATSON   Map: GW 55

On February 27, 1913, P. B. Watson committed suicide, shooting himself through the heart. The *Park Record* reported that he had been having "domestic troubles," and had been in a deep depression. Although he had recently moved to Salt Lake City, Watson had been employed as a stone mason and cement worker at the King Coalition mine.

Watson left a suicide note, addressed to his "Dear daughter," in which he left his house at 324 E. Sixth South in Salt Lake to her. He also added with a "P.S.", that he was bequesting his gold watch to her. This watch had belonged to his 11-year-old son, James, who had died of heart trouble. Watson closed by saying, "It took a hard effort to write this, as I am so nervous. I love you till the last." Watson was laid to rest by his son's side.

EDWIN C. WILLIAMSON

Map: GW 15

Edwin was one of the town's druggists. His ads for pharmaceutical products filled the pages of the local newspaper in the early 1890s -- *DeWitt's Salve and Chamberlain's Cough Remedy* promised cures for almost any problem you had. Williamson lived to the age of 62, dying in 1899. It's believed his father, Jonathan, who died in 1886 at the age of 82, is buried in the same plot.

JOSEPH ZUCCA   Map: GW 11

As if life in the mines wasn't dangerous enough, living in the valleys during the winter could be quite hazardous. There were scores of people killed or injured in avalanches that swept down the mountainsides without warning.

It was March 7, 1897, when the avalanche crashed into the Daly Mine bunkhouses as the miners slept. A total of four men were killed and many injured. Zucca, who was only 27, had been carried around 200 feet and was pinned in the rubble. He was single and had a brother living in town.

In 1894 the *Park Record* printed this poem written by Frank and Alice Robb when their one-year-old daughter died:

One more home is sad and lonely,
One dear face is cold and still;
Where among the angels and God only,
Sought our darling at His will.

The dead are like the stars by day,
Withdrawn from mortal view,
But Thou, O God, has taught us thus to say,
She only sleeps to die no more.

Helena, thou art gone before us,
Where thy little form has flown,
There the tears are wiped away forever,
And sorrow and parting are unknown.

Thou art resting now, our darling,
On thy Heavenly Father's breast;
Where the wicked cease to trouble,
And the weary are at rest.

There within the grave we laid it,
By its little cousin's side,
Who but one short week before it
Joined with the angels to abide.

— *The baby was buried in City Cemetery.*

A GLIMPSE INTO PARK CITY'S HISTORY

1869- UINTAH MINING DISTRICT ORGANIZED.

1872- GEORGE AND RHODA SNYDER MOVED TO PARK CITY.

1872- THE FIRST STAGE LINE BETWEEN SALT LAKE CITY AND PARLEY'S PARK WAS INAUGURATED.

1875- THE FIRST SCHOOL WAS OPENED JUST BELOW ONTARIO MINE. A DANCE WAS HELD ON ST. PATRICK'S DAY TO RAISE MONEY FOR THE DESKS.

1878- THE MASONIC LODGE HAD ITS FIRST MEETING, BUT DIDN'T RECEIVE A CHARTER UNTIL 1880, WHEN IT BECAME UINTAH LODGE NO. 7.

1879- PEARLE SNYDER DIED, AND CITY CEMETERY WAS ESTABLISHED.

1880- *PARK RECORD* NEWSPAPER BEGAN PUBLICATION.

1881- THE CATHOLIC CHURCH WAS BUILT. IT HAD THE LARGEST MEMBERSHIP IN PARK CITY.

1881- PARK CITY RECEIVED TELEPHONE SERVICE.

1881- LARGE TYPHOID EPIDEMIC CLAIMED MANY LIVES.

1882- A LARGE FIRE DESTROYED MANY HOUSES AND BUSINESSES.

1882- A LOCAL DEBATING SOCIETY WAS ORGANIZED.

1883- THE METHODIST MINISTER HELD SERVICES IN A SALOON, SINCE THERE WASN'T A METHODIST CHURCH IN TOWN UNTIL 1884.

1883- THE AMATEUR ATHLETIC ASSOCIATION WAS ORGANIZED.

1884- THE BASEBALL CLUB AND THE PARK CITY BRASS BAND WERE BOTH ORGANIZED.

1885- THE FIRST LOCAL RACETRACK WAS OPENED.

1885- A.M.B. SMITH DIES AND BECOMES FIRST PERSON BURIED AT GLENWOOD CEMETERY.

1885- THE DALY MINING CO. WAS ORGANIZED.

1886- (JANUARY) ONE OF THE HEAVIEST WINTERS EVER SEEN HIT TOWN. SNOW SLIDES KILLED SEVERAL PEOPLE IN THE CANYONS.

1886- WASHINGTON SCHOOL, A LARGE STONE BUILDING, WAS OPENED.

1886- SALOONS WERE REQUIRED TO CLOSE ON SUNDAYS.

1886- THE UNION STATION WAS COMPLETED.

1887- THE LDS CHURCH WAS ORGANIZED. MEETINGS WERE HELD IN THE ROY MERCANTILE STORE, AND BAPTISMS WERE PERFORMED AT THE KILFOYLE RANCH.

1887- THERE WERE MORE THAN 500 STUDENTS ENROLLED IN LOCAL SCHOOLS.

1888- THE LIZZIE EVANS DRAMATIC CO. PERFORMED IN SOCIETY HALL.

1888- BOTH SMALLPOX AND DIPHTHERIA EPIDEMICS LEAVE MANY DEAD.

1888- A 1,500-FOOT DRAINAGE TUNNEL WAS CONSTRUCTED AT THE ONTARIO NO. 3--A MODERN DAY ENGINEERING MIRACLE.

1889- THE FIRST ELECTRIC LIGHTS WERE TURNED ON IN PARK CITY'S BUSINESSES.

1891- THE EQUITABLE WATCH CLUB WAS FORMED AT WISEMAN'S JEWELRY STORE (PARKITES WERE CRAZY ABOUT CLUBS).

1891- "LITTLE LORD FAUNTLEROY" WAS PLAYING AT THE OPERA HOUSE. REFORMED OUTLAW FRANK JAMES, WAS SCHEDULED TO APPEAR SOON, DEMONSTRATING FANCY DRAWS AND MARKSMANSHIP.

1892- THE ENTIRE NATION SUFFERED UNDER THE EFFECTS OF A DEPRESSION. SILVER PRICES DROPPED DRAMATICALLY.

1892- THE GRAND BALL WAS HELD AT THE OPERA HALL. TICKETS COST $1.50 A COUPLE.

1895- THE CIRCUS CAME TO TOWN, COMPLETE WITH A MONSTER MUSEUM, THE STRONGEST MAN ON EARTH, SEA LIONS, GIANT AFRICAN OSTRICHES, AND CAMELS.

1896- UTAH BECAME A STATE. PARK CITY HAD A POPULATION OF OVER 7,000.

1896- A BASEBALL GAME WAS TO BE HELD BETWEEN THE ATHLETIC ASSOCIATION AND THE MINERS' UNION TEAM.

1897- DR. AVID HAD A SERUM WHICH SAVED MANY LIVES WHEN ANOTHER DIPHTHERIA EPIDEMIC STRUCK TOWN.

1897- SILVER PRICES DROPPED SHARPLY AGAIN, SHUTTING DOWN MANY SMALL MINES. MANY MEN WERE LAID OFF.

1898- CONGRESS DECLARED WAR ON SPAIN AND MANY PARK CITY BOYS WERE INDUCTED. THE WAR DROVE UP SILVER PRICES AGAIN.

1898- HIGH SCHOOL WAS STILL BEING HELD IN THE ATTIC OF LINCOLN SCHOOL.

1898- THE "GREAT FIRE" DESTROYED MUCH OF THE CITY.

1900- THE RIO GRANDE'S FIRST STANDARD GAUGE RAILROAD ARRIVED.

1901- (JUNE) WITH GRADUATION NEAR, BOY'S SUITS WITH SHORT PANTS AND A JACKET WERE ADVERTISED. MILITARY STYLE "LITTLE MEN'S SUITS" WERE VERY POPULAR.

1902- THE TOWN'S WORST MINING DISASTER OCCURRED AT THE DALY-WEST, KILLING 34 MINERS. MINE OWNERS PAID FOR THE BURIALS OF THE MINERS WHO HAD NO FAMILIES.

1904- MINERS' HOSPITAL OPENED IN PARK CITY.

1905- THE JUNIOR BASEBALL TEAM WON THE STATE CHAMPIONSHIPS.

1907- A DEADLY WINTER STORM BURIED THE TOWN. MINES HAD TO SHUT DOWN. MONEY BECAME SO TIGHT THAT DAYSHIFT POLICE WERE LAID OFF.

1907- THE NEW CITY ADMINISTRATORS WERE ELECTED. THEY SHUT DOWN SOME OF THE OLD GAMBLING HOUSES, AND THE RED LIGHT DISTRICT WAS MOVED A MORE "RESPECTABLE" DISTANCE FROM TOWN. FINES OF $40 FOR THE MADAMS AND $20 FOR EACH OF THE GIRLS WERE LEVIED PERIODICALLY, KEEPING CITY COFFERS FILLED.

1909- MAPLE HALL BURNED. THIS HAD BEEN THE SITE OF PARK CITY'S FINEST DANCE AND CONCERT HALL, WHICH OFTEN FEATURED THE SALTAIR ORCHESTRA AND THE MOZART ORCHESTRA OF PROVO.

1909- SKIING WAS BECOMING A POPULAR PAST TIME, AND THERE WAS ALREADY SKIING ON TREASURE MOUNTAIN.

1909- THE EDITOR OF THE *PARK RECORD* WROTE: "LITTLE PUFFS OF POWDER, LITTLE DABS OF PAINT, MAKE THE HOMELY MAIDEN, SEEM LIKE WHAT SHE AIN'T."

1910- THE POLICE RAIDED ONE OF THE OPIUM PARLORS IN CHINA TOWN.

1910- GAMBLING WAS FINALLY ABOLISHED.

1912- CEMENT WALKS WERE FINALLY CONSTRUCTED.

1912- SEXTON GIDLEY RESPONDED TO ALLEGATIONS THAT THE CEMETERIES WEREN'T BEING MAINTAINED PROPERLY. HE COMPLAINED THAT THE DOGS WHICH WERE BEING BROUGHT IN FOR WALKS HAD BEEN DOING MORE HARM THAN ANYTHING ELSE.

1913- G. D. JUSTRITE ADVERTISED CORSETS FOR $1.00 TO $5.00.

1913- THE GIRL'S BASKETBALL TEAM PLAYED AN EXCITING GAME AT RASBAND'S HALL. (RASBAND OWNED THE DEWEY THEATER)

1914- THE WAR IN EUROPE (WORLD WAR I) HAD CAUSED METAL PRICES TO RECOVER. PROSPERITY SLOWLY RETURNED TO TOWN.

1914- TWO "AUTO-STAGE" LINES OPENED BETWEEN PARK CITY AND SALT LAKE CITY. THE S&K WAS OWNED BY JOHN SWEATFIELD AND ROBERT KIMBALL.

1916- THE ROOF OF THE DEWEY THEATER COLLAPSED UNDER THE WEIGHT OF SNOW.

1917- DRAFT REGISTRATION FOR THE WAR CAME TO PARK CITY.

1917- PROHIBITION CAME TO PARK CITY TWO YEARS EARLIER THAN THE REST OF THE COUNTRY.

1918- THE WORLD-WIDE SPANISH INFLUENZA EPIDEMIC STRUCK.

1919- WITH THE WAR OVER, METAL PRICES SLIPPED AGAIN, AND PARK CITY'S ECONOMY SUFFERED. THE UNIONS CALLED A STRIKE, AND THE MINES WERE CLOSED.

1919- WAR VETERANS MET AT ELKS HALL IN APRIL AND ESTABLISHED ONE OF THE NATION'S FIRST AMERICAN LEGION POSTS.

1922- THE UTAH SKI CLUB MET IN PARK CITY. A SKI JUMP HAD BEEN OPENED ON TREASURE HILL.

1922- THE *PARK RECORD* WARNED AUTO DRIVERS THAT THE SPEED LIMIT IN TOWN WAS 15 MPH.

1923- THE NEW EGYPTIAN THEATER OPENED ON THE SITE OF THE OLD DEWEY THEATER.

1926- A LABOR DAY CELEBRATION WAS HELD NEAR THE SPIRO TUNNEL, COMPLETE WITH FREE DRINKS AND REFRESHMENTS, AND $1,600 IN PRIZES.

1929- (OCTOBER 29) BLACK FRIDAY. THE BEGINNING OF THE GREAT DEPRESSION. THE LATE 1920S HAD BEEN BOOM YEARS IN PARK CITY. THE POPULATION WAS BACK UP TO 4,200. AFTER THE CRASH, HOWEVER, METAL PRICES FELL, AND MEN WERE LAID OFF. A SOUP KITCHEN WAS SET UP IN TOWN TO HELP THE UNEMPLOYED.

1930- THE HIGH SCHOOL PRESENTED "GYPSY ROVER," A MUSICAL, FEATURING 20 "DAMES" IN BLACK COSTUMES WITH SEAMLESS HOSE.

1930- A SARDINE CANAPE RECIPE CALLED FOR SARDINE PASTE ARRANGED ON TOAST ROUNDS WITH STUFFED OLIVES AND A BORDER OF FINELY CHOPPED EGG WHITES. "THEY SHOULD BE SMALL ENOUGH TO BE HELD DAINTILY WITH FINGERS AND NOT EXPECTED TO PROVIDE MORE THAN THREE MOUTHFULS. (PUBLISHED IN THE *PARK RECORD*)

1930- THE *PARK RECORD* PUBLISHED THE LIST OF JURORS FOR THE YEAR. THEY WERE ALL MEN.

1932- BY MARCH THERE WERE 86 LOCAL FAMILIES RECEIVING RELIEF. THE HOOVER CAFE PROVIDED MEALS FOR THE SINGLE MEN IN NEED OF HELP. THE PARK CITY RELIEF COMMITTEE RAISED OVER $7,000 IN AID.

*

Since this book focuses on Park City's pioneers, this abbreviated timetable ends in 1932. Naturally, there have been many ups and downs in Park City's local economy since the 1930s. Silver prices continued to fluctuate, and the mines were eventually closed.

The town has experienced a resurgence in recent years with the growth of the ski industry. Today, Park City boasts of more than 4200 acres of ski terrain. With 64 buildings listed on the National Register of Historic Places, and numerous local festivals, such as Robert Redford's Sundance Film Festival, it's no wonder that Park City attracts visitors from all over the world.

For me, however, Park City will always remain a quiet, unassuming little Victorian mining town.

SOURCES

1900 Utah State Gazetteer and Business Directory, Vol I, 1st Edition, R. L. Polk & Co., Salt Lake City, Utah.

1903-04, 1908-09, 1912-12, & 1914-15 *Utah State Gazetteer and Business Directory*, R. L. Polk & Co., Salt Lake City, Utah.

Biographical Record, Salt Lake City and Vicinity (1902).

Census Records, Summit County, U. S. Census Bureau, 1880 to 1920, on Microfilm, Family History Library, Salt Lake City.

Echoes of Yesterday, Summit County Centennial History, compiled by Marie Ross Peterson, assisted by Mary M. Pearson (1947); published by Daughters of Utah Pioneers of Summit County.

Family Group Records & Pedigree Charts, IGI, Church of Jesus Christ of Latter-Day Saints, Ancestral File Operations, Salt Lake City.

Glenwood Cemetery Registry - provided by the Park City Historical Society.

Lodestar Magazine, Park City, Utah - Numerous articles.

Martin, Phyllis J., *Cemeteries In Summit County*, (1984).

Mountain Memories: A Book of Remembrance, 1848 - 1986; Kamas, Utah Stake of Zion, Church of Jesus Christ of Latter-Day Saints, (1986).

Newbold, Noal C. and Kummer, Bea, *Silver and Snow, The Story of Park City*, Parliament Publications, Salt Lake City.

Park City Cemetery Registry and Map - Computer Diskette and Map provided by Park City Parks and Recreation Dept.

Park City Council Minutes - 1884 - 1985.

Park City Historical Society/Museum - Assorted articles.

Park City Private Sector Records - provided by Park City Parks and Recreation Dept.

Park City Sexton's Cemetery Records, Death and Burial Records, Family History Library, Salt Lake City.

Park Record newspaper, Park City, Utah - Hundreds of issues. On Microfilm at Park City Library.

Police Records - Park City, Utah, 1883 - 1902, and foreward. On Microfilm.

Ringholz, Raye C., *Diggings & Doings in Park City*, Fifth Edition, (1983).

Ringholz, Raye C., *Walking Through Historic Park City*, (1984).

Thompson, George A. and Buck, Fraser, *Treasure Mountain Home*, Park City Revisited; (revised 1993), Dream Garden Press, Salt Lake City, Utah.